Phyllis Schafley - Eagle Fo

Jerry Falwell - Moral Majority

Ed McAteer - Religious Roundtable

Peter B. Gemma - National Pro-Life PAC

Howard Phillips - Conservative Caucus Inc

Nellie Grey - March for Life

ABORTION and
ALTERNATIVES

ABORTION and ALTERNATIVES

Marjory Skowronski

Les Femmes Publishing
Millbrae, CA

Cover design by Brenton Beck

Copyright © 1977 by Celestial Arts

Les Femmes Publishing
231 Adrian Road
Millbrae, CA 94030

First Printing, May 1977

Made in the United States of America

Library of Congress Cataloging in Publication Data

Skowronski, Marjory, 1948 -
 Abortion and alternatives.

 Bibliography: p.
 1. Abortion—United States. I. Title.
HQ767.5.U5S55   301   76-53342
ISBN 0-89087-923-0

  2   3   4   5   6   7   —   82   81   80   79   78

Dedication

Looking with hope
      towards
            the full-flowering of womanhood
as we learn to give birth
      to
      ourselves
      our visions
and only those children
      we consciously and freely choose.

Acknowledgments

While writing this book I met women in the post office, laundromats, grocery stores, and bookstores who shared with me their abortion experiences and encouraged me with their feelings that a book such as this would have been extremely helpful to them during a difficult time.

Many men, too, were very supportive of this work and aware of their own need to understand the implications of abortion more thoroughly.

A special thanks to the women and men who spent hours answering my interview questions on their specific experiences regarding abortion, as well as to the Boston Women's Health Collective who published *Our Bodies, Ourselves*—an invaluable resource.

The following people were especially helpful in providing feedback and specific information since their professional roles gave them a wide range of experience and expertise.

Sharon Nielson and Ian Florian of the Oakland Feminist Women's Health Center; Padma Lampell, Dr. Earl Baxter, Alicia Wang, Beatrice Bostick, Merideth Fuller of the Buena Vista Women's Services; Diane Knuckles and Randy Hollingshead of the Special Care Center; Margo de la Vega, Gene Emery and Maureen Bowen of Kaiser Hospital, Oakland. I am grateful for the time and energy they gave me.

Finally, I would like to send loving Mahalo to my friends: Sandy, Joan, Sally, Donnie, Victor, Barbara, Shanon, Hilda, Ellen, Ellie, who gave me shelter, love, support, inspiration, and the occasional much-needed excuse to take a break and go play.

Table of Contents

Since *Abortion and Alternatives* was first published, there have been new developments in the status of the Hyde Amendment. The following updates information found on pages 4-5.

On June 20, 1977, the Supreme Court ruled on three cases that had a direct impact on the Hyde Amendment, and stated that the "states do not have a financial responsibility to fund elective abortions." On the basis of these rulings, the Supreme Court requested Judge John T. Dooling to reconsider the injunction he had previously issued against the Hyde Amendment. On August 4, 1977, Judge Dooling lifted the injunction. HEW Secretary Joseph Califano ordered the immediate cessation of the use of federal funds for abortions. Since that time, fifteen states have decided to fund abortions for their residents. However, the future of this funding remains in serious doubt.

In December 1977, a somewhat less stringent version of the Hyde Amendment was passed. The Hyde Amendment now provides for the use of federal funds for abortions only under the following conditions:

- The mother's life is in danger.
- A woman has been the victim of rape or incest and the incident was reported promptly to the police or a public service agency.
- Two doctors determine that the mother would suffer "severe and long-lasting physical health damage" without an abortion.

Foreword

Women are going to be free. They are going to determine their reproductive lives as they wish; this is the essence of dignity and personal freedom.

Anne Nicol Gaylor

ABORTION IS ONE OF THE MORE CONTROVERSIAL subjects of our time. Most women may not think very much about this issue until their own situation demands that they do so. Perhaps you have been strongly against abortion, and now find yourself considering one. Maybe you have always supported a woman's right to choose abortion but are not sure you want to exercise that right yourself. "Where do I go?" "What do I do?" "How do I decide?" Maybe these are some of the questions that have entered your mind.

Time is short. To decide nothing is to decide for a continuation of pregnancy. The earlier you have an abortion, the easier it is—physically and mentally. If you choose to continue the pregnancy, the sooner you resolve your feelings about the "unplanned" aspect, and either decide to give up the coming child for adoption or rear the child yourself, the better it will be for both of you.

When a woman feels pressured to make a quick decision, it is often difficult to gather all the information necessary to make a satisfactory and fully informed choice. Although there are already many books written on the subject of abortion, most of them are written by men, and are written from a limited medical, psychological, legal, or moral viewpoint. This book is written in simple language from a woman's viewpoint. I have tried to present the material as objectively as possible. The opinions of professionals and the feelings of women speaking from their own abortion experiences are both presented.

I have based this book on the premises that knowledge dispels confusion, that taking responsibility for ourselves removes defeat, and that growth can emerge from what appears to be the grimmest of circumstances. The decision to have a child or not is yours alone.

I only hope to enhance the quality of your choice.

No matter what a woman decides to do concerning her unwanted pregnancy, the very confrontation with the choice itself
contains within it the demand that you make a choice and take responsibility for it. Often, this is the first time a woman has had to
make a major decision that will so intimately affect her own body,
happiness and life. Although the focus of this book is on the individual woman in the process of choosing her course of action in
response to an unwanted pregnancy, this book is written with the
following five other groups of people in mind.

• Women who have already decided on abortion but who have
some questions or are confused by any of the physical or psychological aspects. For some women, deciding to have an abortion is a
simple procedure. This is almost always because they have thought
about this issue before, and very clearly value remaining childless
at that time. Now that abortion is safe and legal it is more common
for a woman to choose abortion, follow through on her choice, and
continue on with her life. And yet, one readjustment is still necessary—choosing a more effective means to prevent future unwanted
pregnancies. Many times this post-abortion decision is not a simple
one. To avoid the need for a future abortion the issue of prevention
with all of its physiological and emotional dimensions must be met.

• Women who have had abortions and still experience lingering
doubt, sadness, confusion or guilt concerning any aspect of the experience. Because the social climate surrounding abortion has been
primarily a negative one, many women have taken on these negative feelings and have been punishing themselves for abortions
which occurred years ago. Perhaps a woman was pushed to have
an abortion by a parent, husband, or boyfriend and only realized
later that it was not her real choice. On the other side a woman
may feel very relieved and happy after an abortion and then wonder, "Is this okay?" Unfinished emotional business can affect our
present lives. Since abortion is closely linked with our sexuality and
our feminine role, it is important we resolve any lingering conflicts
to make room for greater self-fulfillment and more rewarding relationships with others.

• Men who are in any way participating in a woman's choice to
have an abortion. Although men cannot experience a pregnancy as
a body-event, a man is often deeply involved emotionally. A man
may want the woman to continue her pregnancy even if she

doesn't. Or a man may realize that his refusal to participate in childrearing is the primary influence on a woman's decision to abort. A couple may equally participate in the actual decision but it is still the woman, alone, who must experience the actual operation. How can a man give support and caring to a woman at this time? How does a man take care of his own unresolved feelings concerning the abortion? Many interviews with men have been carried out to create a broad experiential basis for discussion. These will be discussed in Chapter 9.

• Parents and friends of women considering abortions. Although such people are legally as powerless as husbands and boyfriends, they are capable of supporting a woman's right to choose or using their influence to persuade a woman in one way or the other. A woman often needs someone to listen to her as she feels and thinks her way through to a decision. If a parent or friend can "be there" to allow a woman the space she needs to come to a decision by herself, this is extremely valuable.

Caring and compassion, however, are not always enough. When deciding what to do concerning an unwanted pregnancy a woman needs practical information as well. Also, the strong feelings that parents and friends have concerning abortion and the other alternatives will be felt even if they don't verbalize them. If their prejudices are strong, then perhaps they are founded on limited information. The more a person knows about abortion the more difficult it is to hold the opinion that abortion is always the best or worst choice for every woman. Allowing a woman who is dear to you to make a decision that may be difficult or bear unknown consequences is not easy, but infringing on a woman's right to choose for herself is less respectful of her and unhealthy for your relationship with her.

• Professionals advising women who have had or will have abortions are sometimes restricted by their own pro or con bias. Abortion is not simply a medical procedure, nor need it be a deep psychological trauma. The attitudes of professional people who perform and assist in the abortion have an influence on a woman since her position at this time is a particularly vulnerable one. Some professionals with a great deal of experience in this field are very compassionate until a woman admits that she used no birth control or has had a previous abortion. Does a woman who has knowingly risked an unwanted pregnancy need psychological help? My own view is that unplanned pregnancies are just one symptom of a cultural conflict regarding sexuality, motherhood, and the role of women. Institutional policies and professional procedures are sometimes encouraging the unwanted pregnancy syndrome. There is more involved in preventing future unplanned pregnancies than merely including birth control information as part of the abortion procedure. Wanting to help and not knowing how can be frustrating. Perhaps these pages can give you some new alternatives.

The scope of this book includes the medical, legal, moral, religious, historical, philosophical, and psychological aspects of abortion as they relate to a woman facing this option. Many of the generally accepted ideas against abortion are founded on myth, hearsay, or faith. Much of this is now changing, as reflected in the mass media and public opinion polls which favor a woman's right to choose. This does not mean that abortion is always the "right" choice for every woman. When faced with an unwanted pregnancy a woman can choose not to give birth, or she can arrive at a new relationship with the pregnancy which makes it a "wanted" pregnancy. In this book, I have attempted to present the full range of choices available to a woman, including the differing views on abortion, in the hope of providing a firm foundation for a woman's right to choose what *she* most wants to do. Furthermore, I have explored the many possible ways to prevent *future* unwanted pregnancies and to weave abortion into the larger fabric of our sexual-moral beliefs. Finally, I have projected what impact there is and will be on society by the one million American women choosing abortion each year.

CHAPTER ONE

Abortion
and the Law

> *The first rudiments or germen of the human body is not a hu-*
> *man creature, if it be even a living one, it is a foundation only*
> *upon which the human superstructure is raised.*
> *Samuel Farris*
> Elements of Jurisprudence *(1787)*

ON JANUARY 22, 1973, the United States Supreme Court announced
their seven to two decision on the *Roe v. Wade* and *Doe v. Bolton*
cases: during the first trimester of pregnancy a State cannot regulate abortions; during the second trimester the State can regulate
abortion procedures only to preserve and protect a woman's
health; during the third trimester the State can regulate or prohibit
all abortions except those necessary to protect a woman's life or
health.[1] This ruling applies equally to all women, married, and
unmarried, adults and minors.

These decisions were based on rights enumerated in the Constitution. These rights to privacy are upheld by the Fourteenth
Amendment, the rights of the people are protected by the Ninth
Amendment, and the right to freedom of conscience is guaranteed
by the First Amendment.

The Fourteenth Amendment states, " . . . nor shall any State
deprive any person of life, liberty, or property, without due process
of law . . . " Within the language of the Constitution, the Supreme
Court ruled that a fetus cannot be equated with a "person." The
common understanding of that term based on English common

1

law was that the beginning of human life in utero was not yet a human person. Viability is the point at which a fetus becomes capable of living outside the uterus.[2]

The medical definition of abortion is the termination of pregnancy prior to the stage of viability. A woman is a "person" according to Constitution definition, and if she is denied an abortion in the name of the fetus, her own rights would be denied.

The Ninth Amendment was framed to ensure that the States could not usurp the rights of the people too numerous to name specifically in the Constitution. In the case of *Rowe v. Wade*, the Supreme Court held that these Ninth Amendment rights were broad enough to allow a woman to decide whether or not to terminate her pregnancy. The court, however, in its opinion delivered by Justice Harry A. Blackmun, also maintained that this right is not absolute, and "that at some point the State interests as to protection of health, medical standards, and prenatal life become dominant." The Court, therefore, decided that the State may not regulate first trimester abortions. After the first trimester, "a State may regulate the abortion procedure *to the extent that the regulation reasonably relates to the preservation and protection of maternal health*" (italics added).[3] Only at the beginning of the third trimester does a State have a legitimate interest in protecting potential life, and after that point may legally restrict abortions only for the preservation of the life and health of the mother.

With respect to all abortion legislation, the Court also recommended that laws be "narrowly drawn to express only the legitimate State interests at stake."[4]

Abortion is not a question of law as much as it is a question of morals. Freedom of conscience is upheld by the First Amendment. Restricting a woman's right to abort is essentially restricting her right to religious, moral, and conscientious freedom.

In the first trimester of pregnancy, the decision to have abortion is made by a woman with her physician. The State may not regulate first trimester abortions in any way. Just as a patient cannot be legally forced either to have, or not have, an abortion, so too, a physician in private practice cannot be compelled to perform an abortion or even refer a patient to another physician who would. A pregnant woman's right to an abortion and freedom of conscience is of equal importance as a physician's right to freedom of conscience and to perform a medically appropriate treatment.

Second trimester abortions are more dangerous to a woman's life and health and therefore the State has an interest in protecting her. All regulations on second trimester abortions must be reasonably related to protecting the woman. This ability of states to regulate second trimester abortions has the potential to be used to unnecessarily restrict a woman's ability to obtain second trimester abortions. Examples of requirements a State may impose for second trimester abortions are for the physician who is to perform the abortion, requirements concerning the facility in which the abortion may be performed, (whether it is a hospital, clinic, or other facility) and the licensing of that facility. States *cannot* require a woman be a resident of the state in which the abortion is performed, that the abortion be approved in advance by a hospital staff abortion committee, that other physicians also confirm the decision of the attending physician, or that a hospital be accredited by the Joint Commission on Accreditation of Hospitals.[5]

Only at the onset of the third trimester does a State have a legitimate right in protecting potential life. During the third trimester, States may regulate abortions to only those cases which clearly represent a threat to the woman's life or health.

The Supreme Court refused to rule on the difficult question of at what point life begins, or on the personhood or non-personhood of the unborn fetus.

> When those trained in the respective discipline of medicine, philosophy, and theology are unable to arrive at any consensus, the Judiciary at this point in the development of man's knowledge is not in a position to speculate as to the answer.[6]

In June, 1975, the Supreme Court, in its opinion written by Justice Harry A. Blackmun, prohibited State requirements that a husband must consent to a wife's abortion and that a parent must consent to an unmarried minor's abortion. The Court ruled that both these consents are unconstitutional and limit a woman's right to a free choice. This decision settled one of the major questions left by the 1973 ruling.[7]

Abortion is being kicked about as a political issue. Presently, anti-abortionists in government are attempting to limit a woman's choice through various restrictions. Some states still have unconstitutional, restrictive rules on their books which have not yet been challenged. Some anti-abortion groups advocate federal legislation restricting abortion or allowing states to individually regulate the issue. This legislation would have to be in the form of a Constitutional amendment since the Supreme Court has already held that the rights granted to us by the Constitution are broad enough to include the abortion decision. This would, in effect, eliminate a specific right granted by our Constitution. "Success in a strategy of withdrawing by Constitutional amendment a right that the Supreme Court has found to be part of the Bill of Rights would establish a precedent which could be the forerunner of additional successful efforts to compromise or to take away other rights that prove to be unpopular or difficult to enforce."[8]

The equal rights of all women under the law can only be upheld by the legalization of abortion, since restrictive abortion laws have always been successfully evaded by women who had the money to do so. Statistics show that it is the poor women, (who, disproportionately, are of racial and ethnic minorities), who suffer most from anti-abortion legislation. Either a poor woman is forced to bear a child she is not able to care for, or she risks her own life and health by self-induced abortion techniques or those of a backroom abortionist. In 1965, Harlem Hospital admitted 1,054 women for aftercare following incomplete abortions. After the legalization of abortion in 1971, such incidents dropped to 292.[9]

The Hyde Amendment, a bill which would prohibit national funds from being spent for abortions through Medicaid has recently been enacted. Judge John T. Dooling of the New York Federal Court issued a preliminary injunction against this bill, and ordered the Department of Health, Education, and Welfare to continue nationwide reimbursements for abortion services. Medicaid payments for abortion services are continuing pending the outcome of the decision of the courts. This bill would, in effect, deny access to proper health care and abortion services to millions of women living at or below the poverty level, while abortion services would remain readily available to those able to pay.

The legalization of abortion continues to have meaning only if the Department of Health, Education, and Welfare, through Medicaid (federally funded medical assistance for the financially needy) continues to cover the 300,000 abortions per year it presently subsidizes. That's one third of all the abortions performed per year. It is interesting to note that President Carter's appointee to head the Department of Health, Education, and Welfare, Joseph

Califano, is against abortion. Although Secretary Califano has stated he will uphold the law, what effect this will have on the distribution of Medicaid fund for abortion services for needy women is as yet undeterminable.

A poor woman's freedom rests on her right to privately make her own choices regarding reproduction. If our social system locks certain women into poverty-level existence, either by forcing them to have a child they cannot afford to support, or by denying them an abortion because they cannot afford to obtain one, then their freedom to decide whether to reproduce or not is inherently denied. Discontinuing Medicaid payments for abortions for financially needy women would deny to poor women a health service readily available to the rich. Correcting economic injustices rather than eliminating abortion helps any woman, be she poor or rich or in the middle, to practice free choice.

Public hospitals have sometimes refused to allow abortions to be performed in their facilities. Courts have stated that public hospitals supported by public funds and administered by public employees must permit willing physicians on their staff, or those with staff privileges to perform abortions if they offer analogous ob-gyn services. The issue is still being decided as to whether or not a public hospital (with ob-gyn services) must provide alternative abortion services to the community or hire new staff who are willing to perform abortions if none of its staff is willing to do so. The courts maintain the position that they will not regulate the policies of private hospitals. The refusal or uncooperative attitude of hospital personnel and administration presents a more formidable barrier to women seeking second trimester abortions. Many women have only one hospital in their vicinity and are therefore forced to travel to another location to have their abortion needs met.

The history of the United States anti-abortion legislation began with the Connecticut law of 1821, which restricted abortion because of the great risk to a woman's health it presented at that time. Prior to this law, abortion was an accepted practice under English common law, although the techniques were often crude and hazardous.

The continued illegal status of abortion, over the past 50 years at least, has obviously been entangled with other issues besides a woman's health. Other issues intimately related to abortion are the rights of women, and the philosophical, medical, and/or religious opinions which deem the fetus is a human person.

A first trimester abortion became a safe medical operation in the 1920s. Mortality rates for illegal abortions are significantly higher than for medically safe, legal abortions.

The right to control our fertility began in 1937 when the dissemination of birth control information by doctors became legal in this country. One strong woman, Margaret Sanger, who coined the word "birth control," almost single-handedly won this right for women. Ms. Sanger, who came from a Catholic family, wrote in her book, *My Fight for Birth Control*:

> Constantly I saw the ill effects of childbearing in women of the poor. Mothers whose physical condition was inadequate to combat disease were made pregnant, through ignorance and love, and died. Children were left motherless, fathers were left hopeless and desperate, often feeling like criminals, blaming themselves for the wife's death—all because these mothers were denied by law knowledge to prevent conception.[10]

There are still many states who have similar laws on their books preventing birth control information from being given to minors. Less than forty years have passed since Margaret Sanger won for women the right to plan their motherhood. She devoted her energies for more than fifty years to this work, and in the process faced jail sentences, exile, and social ostracism. She bravely met these obstacles and not only overcame them, but applied her creative energy to establishing the first contraceptive clinic in this country and founding American Planned Parenthood.

Abortion is now the second most common surgical procedure (after tonsillectomy). In 1974, 900,000 women had abortions. Two-thirds of these women were under 25 and three-fourths of them were unmarried. The 1975 figures are estimated on one million. About 70 percent of these abortions would have been performed even if abortions had remained illegal. There are still, however, many late abortions being performed because women encounter difficulty in exercising their right to choose. It is estimated that one-third to one-half of the women who want abortions cannot get them. This is particularly true for young women. Three-fourths of the late abortions are performed on women 15 years and younger. Thirteen states still have no abortion clinics. Twenty-six states have only a few clinics in their big cities. Public hospitals are delaying in offering this health service. Only 30 percent of group-insurance policy holders are covered for abortion according to a survey by the Health Insurance Association.

Clearly the fight for a woman's right to choose is not over. Appendix I gives a list of organizations which are fighting this and other such bills aimed at restricting a woman's right to choose abortion.

CHAPTER TWO

Differing Perspectives on Abortion

I hold everything sacred. I hold the knowing of the world so sacred that I take every chance to make it more accurate, to bring it closer to truth. Refusal to question some contradiction in my understanding of reality means that I do not respect my view of things enough. A view that I have questioned mercilessly merits far more reverence than one that I have never challenged.

Don Juan

ABORTION HAS BEEN WIDELY PRACTICED throughout time and cultures. Knowledge of birth control and abortions dates far back in history. As with all human knowledge, the trial and error method was employed to test the accuracy of the knowledge of the day. Not surprisingly, the availability of such knowledge rose and fell in response to the changing status of women in a given culture. Any viewpoint on abortion does not exist in isolation. The rightness or wrongness of a given act is always based upon a value system which takes into account many factors. The most crucial factor which underlies the abortion controversy today is, "When does the fetus become a person?" How can we decide such a question? Let us look to anthropology, science, religion, research, and our own experience to explore different viewpoints.

Antropology: In 1955, George Devereux published *A Study of Abortion in Primitive Societies*, which analyzed the prevention of birth in 400 pre-industrial societies. His findings and conclusions give us a broad spectrum in which to place our own attitudes about abortion.

Illegitimacy was found to be a reason for abortion only in societies where the mother, the child, or its kin are penalized. Economic reasons for abortion are found to exist in those cultures which will not support more than a certain quota of children, or where children are born under certain circumstances, such as after the death of the father. In some cultures, women have actually aborted their first pregnancy in order to prolong their youthful status and figure. In some nomadic cultures women abort all pregnancies after the birth of two children since more would seriously threaten the survival habits of the tribe. The attitudes toward motherhood seem to vary between cultures in direct relationship to the male attitude toward fatherhood (which is based on the economic usefulness or uselessness of children and the social value placed on the fathering role).

Devereux's view is that every pregnancy, no matter how planned and how joyful, demands certain physiological, psychological, and social adjustments. Likewise, the purposeful interruption of a pregnancy also requires physiological, psychological and social adjustments. Both of these situations ask that the woman respond in some way, and therefore entail a certain amount of "stress." The anthropological data collected indicates that a woman's choice to abort or not to abort is made on the basis of which kind of "stress"—that incurred from abortion or that incurred from continued pregnancy—is less painful for her. The women studied made that choice on the basis of the value system prevalent in their society.

Obviously, social value systems vary widely. Comparing United States abortion statistics with Devereux's findings, it is interesting to note that three-fourths of the women seeking abortions are unmarried. Our culture clearly disfavors childbirth outside marriage. One-third of all abortions performed are paid for by Medicaid and performed on poor women, which coincides with the economic reasons for abortion found in other cultures. Would there be fewer abortions if the social stigma of "illegitimacy" were lifted and all children born would be well-provided for?

Historical: Generally, most historical traditions dealing with abortion and morals are intimately bound to some religion. The positions of the major religions of the world on the question of abortion are mentioned below. It is interesting to note that the source of our own Western civilization, ancient Greece, considered abortion an accepted practice for limiting population. Their view of the common good took into account the numbers of people each social group could sustain and discouraged the birth of any more. The philosophers Plato and Aristotle approved and encouraged abortion. Plato encouraged only healthy and educated people to reproduce. Aristotle felt that a woman who already had all the children she wanted, and those over 40, should have abortions.

Medical: The Oath of Hippocrates states:

> I will give no deadly medicine to anyone if asked, nor suggest any such counsel; furthermore, I will not give to a woman an [instrument] to produce an abortion.

In researching ancient methods of abortion I found that many of them threatened a woman's life. In my opinion, the mention of abortion in the same sentence as the mention of a deadly medicine suggests that Hippocrates did not consider it ethical to risk a woman's life in procuring an abortion. This is the same reasoning that supported the original anti-abortion laws of the 1900s in the United States. It is fortunate that today we have surgical procedures that are safer and do not present the risk to a woman's life abortion once did.

The Physicians' Forum adopted a statement in 1968 which holds that "every woman has the right to regulate her reproductive life, . . . the decision regarding abortion is a highly individual matter which should be agreed upon by patient and physician . . . abortion is a medical concern." It urges "the repeal of all laws which accept the premise that abortion is a criminal act."[11]

Biological: Although the life sciences have yet to unravel many of nature's mysteries, there are some facts biological research has determined. C. Means holds the position that life is continuous:

> There are a living human sperm and a living human ovum before the moment of fertilization, and all that happens at that moment is that two squads of 23 chromosomes each perform a nimble quadrille on the genetic drill-field and arrange themselves into a platoon of 46. There is no more human life present after this rearrangement than there was before . . . what life there is, is the same as before; it is continuous.[12]

Certainly at conception, all of the genetic information needed to produce a human person is present. All of life is a composite of matter, energy, information and time. Embryologists have posited that about 50 percent of all human conceptions end in spontaneous miscarriages. Each human embryo in its growth process evolves through all the stages of life that occurred prior to the human life form.

The one-celled embryo begins to divide and continues through amazing form changes, becoming fish-like, amphibian-like, reptile-like, bird-like, mammal-like, and finally human.[13] At one month, which is about six weeks after a woman's last menstrual period (denoted by the acronym LMP) the embryo is a pea-sized mass of tissue. Near the end of the second month (10 weeks LMP) the embryo is one inch long, now called a fetus, and is beginning to assume human shape. By three months (14 weeks LMP) a fetus is three inches long and the amniotic sac has grown around the fetus, helping to protect it. Around the 20th week, the fetal heartbeat begins and the woman may feel movements (quickening). Between 24 and 28 weeks the fetus may live (although usually not for long), if a woman has a miscarriage. Shortly before viability (the point at which the fetus may sustain its own life meaningfully outside of the womb) the fetal brain wave patterns become discernible.

RELIGIOUS VIEWPOINTS

The attitudes of the world's religions toward abortion have varied over time. Below, I have tried to present an overview of religious attitudes, both past and present, toward the issue of abortion.

Jewish: Among the Orthodox, Conservative, and Reform branches of Judaism, opinions on abortion vary, but it is never totally condemned. The Orthodox uphold the most restrictive view and the Reform group the most permissive. The Old Testament does not mention abortion, probably because it was not a problem in those days. In the Talmud (Tahorator II, oboloth 7:6) a woman who is having grave difficulty giving birth and would otherwise die is permitted to have the child aborted. If the head had already been delivered then the child's life is of equal value to the mother's and cannot be harmed.

Jewish ensoulment beliefs differ but most references regard viability or birth as the time when the soul enters than conception. In the first 40 days of pregnancy the fetus is considered to be still relatively unformed and in a liquid state. Early abortions are therefore more acceptable for this latter reason as well, because the threat to the mother's health is not great. Jewish law places great emphasis on saving life and health, and the well-being of a pregnant woman is considered a priority. The Union of American Hebrew Congregations in 1967 made the following statement concerning the liberalization of abortion laws:

> We commend those states which have enacted humane legislation in this area and we appeal to other states to do likewise and permit abortions under such circumstances as threatened disease or deformity of the embryo or fetus, threats to the physical and mental health of the mother, rape and incest, and the social, economic and psychological factors that might warrant therapeutic termination of pregnancy.[14]

Roman Catholic: The current position of the Catholic church forbids abortion even in the case where continuing a pregnancy will result in the death of the woman, This position is based on Papal Canon 2350 of 1917 and on the encyclical "Costi Cannubi," written by Pope Pius XI in 1930. This encyclical states that "the life of each [mother and fetus] is equally sacred and no one has the power, not even the public authority, to destroy it." In the same encyclical, birth control is forbidden as an "act against nature." More recently, in 1968, Pope Paul VI stated:

> We must once again declare that the direct interruption of the generative process already begun, and above all, directly willed and procured abortion, even for therapeutic reasons, are to be absolutely excluded as licit means of regulating birth.[15]

His position on the subject has not altered since that time.

Although the Catholic hierarchy is very clear about its official position on abortion, the actions of Catholic women reflect another point of view. The Wisconsin Committee to Legalize Abortion, the first abortion referral group in that state, reports that 75 percent of the women they referred over the four-year period prior to the legalization of abortion were Catholic. The Clergy Consultation Service in Milwaukee, reports that in 1972, 80 percent of the women they referred were Catholic, and in 1973, 70 percent were Catholic. A comprehensive sociological study done at a California abortion clinic found that 35 percent of the women seeking abortions were Catholic—and that percentage reflected the proportion of Catholics in the community.

In December of 1974, the National Opinion Research Center reported that in a survey of American Catholics, 70 percent agreed that a married woman who had decided to limit her family should be able to obtain a legal abortion; 19 percent said they might consider having an abortion themselves; and 8 percent conceded that they would have one themselves.

An organization called Catholics for a Free Choice is comprised of those within the Catholic church who advocate free choice for women and maintain that the abortion decision is the responsibility of the individual woman, not the Church. This organization welcomes membership from people of all faiths.

Protestant: Protestant denominations agreed with the Catholics through the first half of the twentieth century—that abortion was contrary to divine law and should be forbidden. However, in 1961 the National Council of Churches approved hospital abortions "when the health or life of the mother is at stake." Potential life was emphasized and abortion as a method of birth control continued to be condemned.

In 1958, at a conference held by the Protestant Episcopal Church and the Church of England, contraception was approved with no restrictions and abortions approved only to protect a woman's life and health. More recently, the Department of Christian Social Relations of the Episcopal Church acknowledged that abortion is decided among Episcopalians individually, with a woman's own personal moral judgment and that of her family, physician, and parish priest taken into consideration.

The 1968 American Baptist Convention approved of an individual's responsible and personal choice to abort. Some provisions were stated: termination must occur before the twelfth week of pregnancy unless the pregnancy seriously threatens the life or health of the woman, there is a risk that the child would be deformed, or rape or incest was the cause of pregnancy. The convention encouraged their churches to provide "realistic and sympathetic counseling on family planning and abortion." Further study and research was encouraged.

In 1972, the United Presbyterian Church considered abortion a possible decision in regards to saving a woman's life.

In 1968, the general assembly of the Unitarian Universalist Association urged that:

> . . . efforts be made to abolish existing abortion laws, except to prohibit performance of an abortion by a person who is not a duly licensed physician, leaving the decision as to an abortion to the doctor and his patient.[16]

In general, the Protestant churches have attempted to respond to the needs of their people in a changing world.

Quakers: The Society of Friends was founded on belief in a Supreme Power that is good, and the belief that each person has the capacity to respond to this goodness. The Quakers have opposed war, capital punishment, and slavery on the basis of reverence for human life and concern for the quality of life. Throughout the 300 years of its history, the Friends have devoted their efforts to freeing the slaves, reforming prisons and mental institutions and other humanitarian pursuits. In 1969 the American Friends Service Committee published the book *Who Shall Live? Man's Control over Birth and Death* which contains this statement:

> We believe that no woman should be forced to bear an unwanted child. A woman should be able to have an abortion legally if she has decided that this is the only solution she can accept and if the physician agrees that it is in the best interest of mother and child. She should be encouraged to seek the best social and spiritual counseling available before reaching a decision; and the physician, for his own support, should have the opportunity to confer with colleagues of his choosing if he feels the need for such consultation.[17]

Buddhist: "Ahisma" (non-violence) is the main tenet of Buddhism which does not permit the killing of any life-form. Abortion is still as widespread in Buddhist countries as anywhere else. The Japanese, who are mainly Buddhist, have, however, readily accepted abortion due to the influence of Shintoism which holds that a human being is present only at birth, not before.

Muslim: The Grand Mufti of Jordan, in December 1964, stated "It is permissable to take medicine to procure abortion so long as the embryo is unformed in human shape." The unformed state was considered to continue for 120 days after conception. Life begins in the fetus 150 days after conception and before this time is not considered human. The Muslim scriptures do however forbid abortion.

Hindu: In the ancient scriptures of the Atharva-Veda, abortion was clearly condemned. There is a recognition in the code of ethics that the ideal actions which can be expected from the few righteous individuals can not always be followed by the millions of everyday people. One writer, Susruta, of the Ayurveda tradition (which encompasses medical knowledge) approves of early termination of pregnancy when there is a threat to the woman's health. A root herb is mentioned in that text which will induce abortion.

Classical Hindu literature includes three schools of thought regarding ensoulment: 1. that life begins at conception; 2. that life begins at quickening; 3. that life begins at birth with the first breath. Recognition of the continuity of life's cycle through many forms is basic to Hindu belief. Each successive stage of developing life is considered of greater value. The individual is not considered a conscious self until birth. The Hindu belief system is in no way static. In the Gupta period when women gained many rights and became active in political affairs abortions became approved. In modern India the pressing need of her people to control fertility has become a more important issue than traditional religious attitudes. Socio-economic reasons, therefore, are as important, if not overriding factors in determining views on abortion.

It is my own personal opinion that the soul of an individual human person can enter anytime between conception and birth, that the timing is different in each individual situation. The reports of many (50) women I have spoken to who have given birth seems to verify this opinion. Some experience the soul entering at conception, others at about five months, and still others only at birth. There is no way to prove that this opinion is true or false, but perhaps a woman's own intuition is her best guide in this very delicate matter.

The multifaceted aspects of abortion must be understood in order to see how their totality affects a woman's decision concerning whether or not to continue her pregnancy. By including this section on the varying historical, religious, and philosophical views on abortion, I hope to give women some perspective from which to evaluate their feelings and attitudes.

ABORTION IN OTHER COUNTRIES

The legalization of abortion varies from country to country thoughout the world. Below find a partial listing of countries, most of which have at least somewhat liberalized their laws. Some countries such as China, Japan, and Russia grant abortions on request. Countries with a very strong Catholic influence still uphold the most stringent of laws against abortion.

Africa: In most of Africa, abortion is seldom mentioned and remains illegal. In 1975, the South African parliament passed a bill permitting abortion only if a woman obtains certificates of necessity from three doctors. One of the necessities mentioned was the pregnancy resulting from the sexual union of a white and nonwhite which is forbidden by law.

Canada: The liberalized laws permit abortion to protect the life and health (mental and physical) of the woman, but a hospital review board must approve each case. In the more liberal provinces this is treated as a formality. However, the more restrictive provinces use this measure as an obstacle for women seeking abortions.

Red China: Both birth control and abortion are freely available to Chinese women as part of their health service.

France: After long televised debates the French National Assembly noted on November 29, 1947 that abortion on request is legal throughout the first ten weeks of pregnancy, at set prices.

Eastern Europe (that part under Communist control): Shortly after World War II, abortions became legal and free in these countries. However, laws have become more restrictive in countries desiring population expansion, indicating that the right to abortion is determined by the social needs of the country and not by the rights of women.

Great Britain: In 1967, through an Act of Parliament, abortion is permitted if continuation of pregnancy is a greater risk to a woman's physical or mental health than the termination of that pregnancy. The procedure can be done within the first 28 weeks of pregnancy and must be approved by two doctors.

India: The Medical Termination of Pregnancy Act, which was passed in 1971, is one of the most liberal of its kind in the world, in that the failure of contraceptives is included as a valid ground for abortion (but only for the married, unmarrieds don't count).

Israel: Israel has just passed the nation's first legalized abortion law, despite opposition from religious factions. This law will take effect in January of 1978, and will permit abortion in cases of danger to the woman's physical or mental health, rape, incest, likely birth defects and when the mother is unwed.

Italy: The Constitutional Court in 1975 declared the embryo "not yet a person" and decreed that a woman's health and sanity took priority.

Japan: Late in the 1940s Japan liberalized abortion and soon endorsed abortion on request as a measure to control population during their post-war struggle for economic survival. Japan has no tradition of contraceptive use and as recently as 1945, Margaret

Sanger was denied entry to speak on the subject of contraception.

South and Central America: In Argentina, abortion is permitted if the pregnancy seriously jeopardizes a woman's health, or if the fetus is known to be retarded or deformed. The abortion law of Uruguay takes into account a woman's honor, health, rape, and serious economic difficulty. Most of the other Latin countries continue to regard abortion as totally illegal, and illegal abortions abound at the expense of women's health.

Soviet Union: Abortion was first legalized in 1920 and then prohibited under Stalin except for grave medical reasons. In 1955 legal abortions were again reestablished through the first trimester of pregnancy. Russian women are given abortion services as part of their free medical care and given up to 15 days leave from work.

Sweden: In 1938, the first liberalization of the Swedish abortion law, still left many restrictions on the books. January 1975 marked the abolishment of most obstacles and women may now obtain abortion on request through the twelfth week of pregnancy. Some formalities continue to be required for second trimester abortions.

Switzerland: Although rich women have flown to Switzerland from all over Europe and the United States for illegal abortions in luxurious clinics, the Swiss women themselves are still legally denied abortions.

Spain and Portugal: Abortion remains illegal in both these countries.

Middle East: Therapeutic abortions are permitted in Turkey, Iran, Egypt, Morocco and Tunisia. The other Muslim countries which ban abortions seldom enforce their laws.

CHAPTER THREE

Medical Facts
and Uncertainties

*The earlier an abortion is done, the safer it is! Also the less
painful and expensive it will be for you.*

Our Bodies Ourselves

How DO I KNOW for sure I'm pregnant? Who can perform an abortion? Does it hurt? Will I be able to have children later? How long
does it take? Will I be weak afterward? All these and more are
common questions. Knowing the answers to all these practical considerations can often relieve you of the biggest anxiety that arises
when one is thinking of having an abortion—the fear of the unknown.

Determining pregnancy: There are some early signs of pregnancy which appear in some women weeks before a laboratory test
or a pelvic exam can indicate anything. These signs are quite variable, and may become apparent as early as 2-4 weeks after conception. One of these is a bluish tint around the oss, which is the
opening to the cervix. The oss can easily be viewed by using a speculum, mirror, and flashlight. Not all women show this sign and the
only way to be sure there is any change in color from the usual is to
already be familiar with your own cervix through regular self-examination. (Read more about this in the section on self-help.)
Breast swelling and tenderness may occur with a missed menstrual
period. It is important to note, however, that the same symptoms
may occur prior to a normal menstrual period. If a woman has
been pregnant before and knows that is the only time her breasts

19

swell she can question seriously whether or not she is pregnant again. For women using the sympto-thermal method of birth control (described more fully on page 88) an elevated post-ovulatory temperature that stays high for longer than 2 weeks is an excellent indication of pregnancy. The famous morning sickness syndrome may simply indicate anxiety, but can also herald the real thing. Unusual mood swings and a mental haze can accompany the hormonal changes of early pregnancy (or the onset of the flu). Worrying about being pregnant can cause all these symptoms and more. A few women "know" as soon as they become pregnant, without any apparent sign—and they're often proven right.

If a woman, from watching or feeling her bodily changes, is sure she is pregnant she can qualify for a pre-emptive abortion. A pre-emptive abortion is a suction aspiration abortion performed with a small, flexible cannula attached to a suction syringe *before* pregnancy is verifiable by a laboratory test. A pre-emptive abortion is most commonly called menstrual extraction or menstrual regulation.

PREGNANCY TESTS

Most women do not suspect they are pregnant until after they have missed a period. Women who have irregular or long cycles may be six weeks pregnant or more before they have enough reason to think they may be pregnant.

There are several laboratory tests that determine pregnancy. Most public health clinics, Planned Parenthood clinics, feminist health collectives, and private gynecologists do pregnancy testing. The fees vary from free to $8 (for most), and higher for a private gynecologist. The most widely used laboratory test is a urine analysis, which checks for a hormone produced by a woman's body after the onset of pregnancy.

The hormone being tested for is human chorionic gonadotropin (hCG). This hormone begins being produced after conception. Until the 42nd day LMP, hCG does not reach a level high enough to show a positive result on a urine analysis. Though hCG continues to be produced throughout the pregnancy, it reaches its peak level at about 12 weeks LMP. After this time, though hCG is still being produced, it is produced in much smaller amounts, and the level of hCG in the urine drops off slightly.

There are two different types of urine analysis tests. One is a 2-

hour test that is reliable approximately 38 days LMP. The 2-minute slide test is reliable approximately 42 days LMP. Women should be wary of the 2-minute slide test; it is less accurate than the 2-hour test and more often will show a false positive, and indicate pregnancy when the woman is actually not pregnant.

After you have contacted the clinic to which you will be taking a urine specimen there are some important preparations you must make to insure an accurate reading. Do not eat or drink anything after dinnertime the night before. Prepare in advance a very clean, dry jar which can hold about one-half cup of liquid. You will be collecting the first urine of the morning. (For those of us who have to go to the bathroom immediately upon arising, forgetting to prepare the jar in advance can result in a mad scramble to find and clean an appropriate jar before it's too late.) Once you have collected that all-important specimen, it is best to keep it refrigerated until it's time to take it to the clinic. (If you live with other people, it is wise to put the jar in a brown bag and label it.) The results of the test should be obtainable within 24 hours.

If a pregnancy test comes back positive, it usually means you are pregnant. However, it could be a false positive, due to inaccuracy of the 2-minute slide test, menopause could be setting in, or the positive result may be due to a tumor. If it comes back negative, it is still possible you are pregnant. A pregnancy test can give a "false" negative due to contamination of the urine, the urine getting too warm, the concentration of the urine being too weak (which is likely if you got thirsty at midnight and didn't think it would matter if you drank a glass of water). If it is too early in the pregnancy the urine analysis won't be valid because the hormone your body starts secreting at the onset of pregnancy may not have built up sufficiently to register a positive result. If your results come back negative, and your period still hasn't come in another week, go back for another test. *Caution:* some women never receive a positive test result, due to their body chemistry. If your period still does not arrive after two lab tests, you should go to a doctor for the second type of pregnancy test—a pelvic exam. However, a doctor cannot *feel* pregnancy until approximately 6-8 weeks LMP.

When a woman is pregnant her uterus begins to swell from its original size to the size of an orange at about eight weeks after the last menstrual period, to the size of a grapefruit at about twelve weeks. The uterus also becomes softer. Women in advanced self-help groups become skilled in doing pelvic exams and familiar enough with each other's bodies to be able to detect very early swelling. A pelvic exam must be done by a doctor to qualify a woman for an abortion.

For some women this may be their first pelvic. It helps to know what to expect. The doctor will ask you to take your clothes off below the waist, put on a smock or drape and lie down on the examining table with your knees bent and spread out on the sides. The doctor will then insert two gloved and lubricated fingers into your vagina and under the cervix towards the uterus. She or he will then push gently upward while with the other hand presses down on your abdomen. The doctor will feel for the size and consistency of the uterus. This can all be done very gently. If you are tense, the doctor will have a harder time feeling through your tightened muscles. If the doctor is hurting you, speak up, and ask her or him to be more careful. The pelvic only takes a few seconds, and then you will know for sure if you are pregnant and how many weeks along you are.

Once pregnancy is determined, and if the decision is made to abort, the easiest and safest method if you are 7-12 weeks pregnant is a suction-aspiration abortion (also called suction-curettage). For some women, it may be helpful to know what to expect.

METHODS OF ABORTION

Vacuum Aspiration Abortion (Suction Curettage): A vacuum aspiration abortion is done up to 12 weeks LMP. A flexible cannula is used, which insures against uterine perforation, but requires more skill on the part of the physician to remove all the tissue. A general anaesthesia is not given unless a woman asks for it, since such overall relaxation causes the uterine walls to soften and perforation can occur more easily. A woman is sometimes advised to eat breakfast as usual to ward off weakness. Most clinics provide counseling prior to the procedure so a woman will know what to expect during and after the abortion.

As part of the pre-operative procedure you will be asked to fill out a complete medical history so the doctor can be alerted to any possible complications. Blood is taken by needle from the forearm to be tested for the Rh factor, anemia, and sickle-cell trait. Temperature, pulse and blood pressure are taken to make sure you are in good health. Some clinics schedule these tests the day before, along with a laminaria insertion.

Laminaria is a dried stick made of seaweed. Once it is inserted into the cervical oss, it expands slowly as it absorbs moisture. This causes the cervix to dilate gradually. Some doctors believe this method is less painful than manual dilation, done immediately before the abortion. Laminaria should never remain in the oss for more than 12 hours. Currently, medical opinion on the use of laminaria is divided. Planned Parenthood in Inglewood, California seems to favor the use of laminaria with intelligent and aware women who are reliable. They feel it decreases the pain and discomfort of an abortion dilation procedure. The use of laminaria with women who are confused or uncertain about even having the abortion runs a greater risk of complication. In the latter case, laminaria could cause infection from being left in too long, or the woman may not show up for the abortion the next day. Laminaria should be used judiciously. Feminist health collectives advise against its use since the dilation is often uncomfortable and more extensive than necessary and the chances of infection are greater.

Some women find that taking dolomite tablets (calcium-magnesium), which are available at health food stores, is a good pain preventative. Vitamin B complex reduces the effects of stress on the body and aids healing.

If you are receiving counseling, then the following description of the procedure will be explained to you in person. You are always entitled to ask questions and to be treated with kindness.

Some clinics offer a nervous system relaxant which is not usually necessary. If you do not want it, you will have to make that very clear in advance, since it is often given as a matter of course.

The doctor will repeat the pelvic exam to be sure of the uterine size. A speculum is then inserted into the vagina. The speculum is a device for stretching the vaginal walls and holding them open. Careful insertion of the speculum is not painful. If a woman is tense, it may be slightly uncomfortable. If there is discomfort it is important to tell the doctor. The speculum is made of metal and can feel quite cool. An antibiotic is swabbed all around the cervix to prevent infection. Then a local anaesthetic is given, and the woman remains awake during the procedure. If a woman prefers to do without the local anaesthetic due to an aversion to drugs, needles, or just because she feels she will not need it, that should be her choice, but the doctor should inform her fully as to the level of discomfort she may feel before a decision is made. Usually 10 cc of xylocaine is given. Sometimes up to 20 cc is given to be sure there is minimal pain during dilation, but dizziness or ringing in the ears may result and the large dose may not be any more effective than the smaller dose. There are very few nerve endings in the cervix so the needle should be felt less than a shot of novacaine given by the dentist. If a woman feels the local anaesthetic being administered, it will be two small prickly sensations. A clamp is placed on the cervix to keep it from moving around. This can pinch slightly.

The cervix is dilated using graduated instruments which look like bent rods. The smallest one is inserted and then a little larger one and so on until the cervix is dilated as needed. The length of pregnancy determines how much dilation is necessary, since the further along a woman is, the more contents there will be in the uterus. During dilation, the cervical opening (oss) is being stretched and this can cause some cramping. A flexible or non-flexible plastic cannula is then passed through the cervix into the uterus, and the contents are suctioned out. If the pump is electrical it makes a loud noise when turned on. Cramping will occur while the tissue is being removed from the uterine wall by suction. Even if the cramping is painful it usually lasts only a couple minutes, although some cramping may continue for a while after the procedure is over.

Some women feel only mild discomfort during their abortions. Others compare the sensations to menstrual cramping. A number of women report "it hurts, but it's over very quickly." Each woman responds to the pain differently. Some counselors encourage a woman to breathe deeply and exert pressure into the pelvic area by constricting the abdomen when the cramps come. This process relaxes tense muscles and reduces pain. Other counselors prefer to distract a woman and encourage her to think about anything except the abortion and related topics. Their rationale is that keeping her distracted lessens her awareness of discomfort. A third approach is to encourage the woman to breathe deeply while the counselor explains the procedure itself, so that she knows what to expect before it happens. Some women feel that being able to prepare themselves a few seconds in advance for the next sensation enhances their feeling of being in control. It is wise to ask which method of counseling your clinic uses, so that if you prefer another method you can ask for it. All feminist clinics are supportive of a woman getting what she needs during her abortion procedure.

Some other clinics are not always so supportive. Most clinics specializing in first trimester abortions offer some counseling of this kind.

The Oakland Feminist Women's Health Center trains "patient advocates" to accompany a woman who must have her abortion in the hospital either because of possible complications, a request for a general anaesthesia, or the need to have a second trimester procedure. Other women's centers may provide this service as well. This requires a prior arrangement with the doctor and hospital. A "patient advocate" gives a woman support and looks out for her well-being during the procedure.

A woman is asked to rest for at least a half hour following this procedure. During this time her blood pressure and pulse are checked. Some women leave the clinic and continue with their day as usual. Others prefer to rest a day or two before resuming their normal activity. Immediately following an abortion, hormonal changes begin to occur in response to the body's sudden return to its normal state. Not much data is available on this. However, it is likely that post-abortion blues may be directly related to this hormonal adjustment, which may not be noticed until 48 hours after the procedure and may linger for a week or longer.

The vacuum aspiration abortion is a very safe medical procedure, almost three times as safe as childbirth. Complications are rare and less than two women in every 100,000 are likely to die from a first trimester abortion. Possible complications include infection, hemorrhage, perforation of the uterus, and incomplete abortion. All of these require further medical attention. A skilled and experienced physician seldom faces these complications. An extra safety factor is a by-pass valve on the mechanical or electrical pump which makes it impossible to push air back into the uterus. Air embolisms account for some of the few deaths and can be avoided altogether by using pumps equipped with this valve.

If your blood is Rh negative, you should receive a Rhogam shot within 72 hours of your abortion. This is explained fully later in this chapter. The cost of the shot will be in addition to the cost of the abortion procedure itself, which ranges from $80 in some Planned Parenthood clinics to $300 charged by some private physicians. Most clinics charge between $125 and $150. If you have an abortion with anaesthetic it could cost $50-$75 more. Be sure to arrange to have someone drive you home; though it may not be necessary, it is generally a good idea.

Bring a sanitary napkin and belt since some bleeding can be expected (although most clinics and doctors provide napkins). Some women continue to spot on and off for one month; a few hardly bleed at all. Immediately following the abortion it is normal to flow from one to three days, using three to five pads, sometimes soaking them all completely through. Soaking more than four pads is ample cause to call the doctor or clinic to be sure everything is okay. The next menstrual period can be expected within four to seven weeks. If it does not come, call the doctor or clinic.

There are some post-abortion instructions which are important to follow to be sure you heal as quickly as possible and prevent any complications:

1. *Nothing* can be put into the vagina for two to three weeks afterwards, otherwise infection may occur. This includes tampons. Do not take baths, swim, douche, or have intercourse.

2. Some activities, such as swimming, horseback riding, jogging, and any other strenuous activity which could cause bleeding must be postponed for a couple of weeks.

3. For five days following the abortion take your temperature morning and evening with a good thermometer. If your temperature goes above 100.4 degrees two readings in a row then call the clinic or doctor immediately. This may indicate an infection which needs prompt treatment.

4. You may be given an antibiotic as a matter of routine to prevent infection. Some doctors do not approve of this practice since it can mask signs of infection while it continues. If you are taking an antibiotic, do not eat for one hour before or after taking it and avoid dairy products (the calcium prevents the drug from being absorbed into the blood stream). After you are finished with the prescription it is advisable to take some yogurt or acidophilus to restore the normal, helpful bacteria in the stomach that are also killed by the antibiotic. The use of antibiotics may also cause vaginal yeast infections in some women. If this occurs, you should see your doctor.

5. Cramping may persist for a day or so and can be relieved by a heating pad, dolomite, chamomile, red raspberry, mint or comfrey teas. It is not advisable to take aspirin, since aspirin will keep your temperature down and in this way disguise an infection. If cramping becomes worse than it was in the beginning and more

prolonged then call the clinic or doctor.

6. After an abortion a woman is given Methergine or Ergotrate which helps the uterus return to its original size. It must be taken every four hours around the clock, including the middle of the night.

7. If breasts swell, become tender or begin to discharge a watery fluid then ice packs can be applied. Wearing a snug bra may also relieve the discomfort. The breasts should not be massaged at this time, nor should any discharge be squeezed out. If discomfort continues call your doctor or clinic.

8. Birth control counseling should always be part of the abortion aftercare. After an abortion, many women worry about their fertility (therefore, subconsciously risking pregnancy again) and/or feel they won't have sex again for some time. Birth control pills can be started the same night of the abortion, or the next morning. An IUD can be inserted at the time of the abortion, though it may be advisable to wait until the onset of the next menses. A diaphragm can be fitted at the two-week post abortion check-up. (Prior to that time it is unsafe to have intercourse anyway.) It is very important that a woman confront the realities of the risk she takes in not immediately addressing the question of birth control, even if she feels she may never want to have sex again—which is a common feeling at first. Even if a woman has already decided on a method of birth control, hearing about all the options can be informative. A woman *can* get pregnant immediately following an abortion, and should address herself to the problem at once.

9. As general, helpful suggestions, I advise the following: take it easy, be good to yourself, choose a nurturing environment and cheerful company in which to recuperate. Eat nourishing food and be sure you are getting enough vitamins and minerals. Go for some leisurely walks in a quiet place. Get as much sleep as your body needs. Listen to your favorite music. Read a good book. Go to a funny movie.

10. Two weeks after an abortion, a woman must receive a follow-up exam by a doctor or nurse practitioner to insure that everything is okay.

Pre-emptive Abortion: The pre-emptive abortion (endometrial or menstrual aspiration) can be done anytime after the menstrual period is due until verification of pregnancy can be determined, which is usually 4-6 weeks from the start of the last menstrual period. A woman can qualify for this procedure if she has been watching or feeling her bodily changes and is sure she is pregnant. A pregnancy test must show a negative result before a woman can qualify for a pre-emptive abortion (hence, the term pre-emptive).

This procedure can be done by a trained paraprofessional. Usually, the cervix is already naturally dilated if a period is late. A small flexible plastic tube is inserted and the lining of the wall of the uterus is emptied by a suction created by a mechanical or electrical pump. A syringe method has also been developed. To insure safety, this method must have a by-pass valve to prevent air from entering the uterus, which could cause an embolism. A local anaesthesia is not usually needed, although some cramping can be expected.

The procedure takes only a few minutes. The advantage of a pre-emptive abortion is that it is much easier on your body than if you waited longer. Some women have a pre-emptive abortion for religious or moral reasons if they even suspect they may be pregnant. However, most women prefer to be absolutely sure they are pregnant before choosing to endure the discomfort and expense of an abortion. Once a woman decides to terminate her pregnancy, she should make all arrangements as quickly as possible. The earlier an abortion is performed, the easier it is on a woman's body and the lower the fee. The price for a pre-emptive abortion is around $80.

This service is available at a few feminist health clinics. It is not widely available, because most private doctors are unwilling to serve this need without pregnancy verification by a test.

If a woman has Rh negative blood, she should not have a pre-emptive abortion, due to the possibility of undetected Rh sensitization occurring. (The Rh factor will be discussed in greater detail later.)

A woman may feel like resting after a pre-emptive procedure, but will usually feel normal again in anywhere from a few hours to a couple of days.

Very Early Abortion: A very early abortion is performed soon after pregnancy has been determined, up until 7-8 weeks after the last menstrual period. When an abortion is performed this early, the risks are very low—about the same as for a tonsillectomy. It is basically the same procedure as a pre-emptive abortion (little or no cervical dilation and the use of a flexible tube). The only difference is that pregnancy has been verified. If a non-flexible tube is used this early in pregnancy, there can be complications, since the uterus is still quite tight. It is not yet legal for this procedure to be done by a paraprofessional, since pregnancy has been diagnosed and is therefore considered an abortion. In a pre-emptive procedure, pregnancy has not been verified by a test, and it is not proven to be an abortion, but a menstrual aspiration.

Dilation and Evacuation (D & E): Prior to the vacuum suction the D & E was the safest and most widely used method for first trimester abortions. The D & E should no longer be used when the vacuum aspiration is available. However, a late D & E can be done up to 15 weeks LMP. This is the *only* method that can be used at this time (between 12 and 15 weeks LMP) because the uterus is too soft for a safe vacuum suction abortion (perforation can occur too easily), and too early for an induction procedure (to be discussed below). The complications of infection, hemorrhage, and uterine perforation are slightly higher than for vacuum aspiration. More bleeding can be expected following a D & E.

The D & E requires a general anaesthesia and is usually performed in a hospital. Because this procedure is routinely used to correct other disorders such as infertility, excessive menstrual bleeding, and persistent irregularity many doctors are familiar with it. The cervix is dilated as it is preceding the vacuum aspiration abortion and then the uterine lining is carefully loosened with a curette (a metal loop on the end of a long thin handle). The fetal tissue is removed with forceps.

The cost of the D &E is about $450 or higher. A few facilities offer this service between 12 and 15 weeks LMP, which is the only time it should be considered. It is safer, easier and less expensive than waiting 16 weeks for an induction abortion. The aftercare instructions are the same as for the vacuum aspiration.

Induction Method: An induction abortion is a late abortion done between 16 and 24 weeks LMP. It is more costly ($350-$750), more risky (16 fatalities per 100,000), and more painful. It is also more difficult to obtain than a first trimester abortion. Some factors which contribute to the need for a second trimester abortion are: inability to obtain a first trimester abortion; difficulty in ascertaining pregnancy; indecision which was not resolved earlier; the decision to terminate the pregnancy resulted from the results of an amniocentesis which cannot be done until 14 weeks LMP; circumstances including a woman's health, financial status, and relationship with partner may change; avoiding the pregnancy (especially a temptation for unmarried teenagers).

Until recently a saline solution was always used to induce expulsion of the fetus. Now another substance called prostaglandins is sometimes used as well. It is important to know the advantages and disadvantages of each so you can choose which one you prefer. The doctor more than likely has a preference as well. Second trimester abortions are subject to state regulations.

Both solutions are used in the same way. A section of the abdomen is cleaned and numbed with a local anaesthetic. Then a large needle is inserted which draws out some amniotic fluid. Through the same needle one of the solutions mentioned above is injected into the amniotic sac. Especially with the saline infusion, great care must be taken to avoid getting salt into the blood vessels which could cause shock and death. It is common to feel bloated, thirsty, and have a headache after this procedure. Any feelings of dizziness, backache, or heat waves should be mentioned to the physician immediately.

The next phase of the induction abortion is waiting. With saline solution contractions will begin between 8 and 24 hours later. With prostaglandins, the contractions will begin sooner. At first the cramping is slight, and then begins to increase. No general anaesthesia is given, since the process could not continue. Pain medication and tranquilizers should be offered. Breathing techniques such as those done with full-term labor can be helpful.

In most cases, the fetus and placenta will be expelled within 18-24 hours with the use of prostaglandins and within 24-36 hours with use of saline infusion.[18] Your hospital stay will continue for twenty-four hours.

Complications with the saline induction include: risk of salt entering the blood vessels, which could be fatal; retention of the placenta, which would necessitate an immediate D & E; hemorrhage at the time of expulsion; or infection later on. Complications with prostaglandins include significantly higher rates of nausea and diarrhea, higher rate of unsuccessful instillations (the instillation was made, but an abortion did not result), excessive bleeding and retained placentas. The cervix may tear due to rapid expulsion. Laminaria insertion can prevent this. The advantage of prostaglandins is that the induction-abortion interval is much shorter. Induction abortions using prostaglandins have, in the past, been felt to be safer than saline instillations. Recent literature, however seems to show a higher rate of complications, both major and non-major, with the use of prostaglandins.[19]

Aftercare procedures are the same as for a vacuum aspiration abortion. The healing process may take longer and a woman should plan to take it easy for at least a week afterwards. The hormonal readjustment may even be more dramatic than it is following a first trimester abortion, so some depressed feelings are not unusual.

Finding a hospital which does late abortions can be difficult. Often hospital staff and boards are opposed to late abortions. Certainly, they are more difficult on a woman than are early abortions. Usually a woman seeking a late abortion is already emotionally exhausted and needs support as well as good medical attention. A few small hospitals specialize in second trimester abortions. General hospitals which offer a special unit, staff, and counseling for late abortions are good. It is important to call a hospital and ask them about their policies beforehand. You may want a "patient advocate" from a woman's center to accompany you. She can prevent any unkind or insensitive treatment from occurring.

Hysterotomy: Very rarely an induction method cannot be performed due to a woman's health condition. Sometimes the induction method is unsuccessful. Major surgery, called hysterotomy, (not to be confused with hysterectomy) is then done. This procedure is used *only* when other methods have failed or when complications are present. This use of this major procedure is *not* acceptable for routine termination of a mid-trimester pregnancy. The fetus is removed through caesarean section. This method is most expensive, $1,000 or more, and most dangerous. The reproductive system is left intact.

Future Childbearing: A woman's fertility is usually unaffected by an abortion. In fact immediately after an abortion, a woman can become pregnant and should be very careful to use birth control. Most of the women who have lost their fertility through abortion have been those who submitted to the techniques of illegal abortionists. A recent study done in England concluded that, although women who had had previous legal abortions tended to have slightly shorter pregnancies, 73.5 percent of the group studied carried their pregnancy to term. No evidence was found that these children were smaller or weighed less than normal.[20] Other complications which may be related to previous abortions are tubal pregnancy, and difficulties in delivery. Teenagers bear as great a risk from abortion as they do from pregnancy. Both of which increase the likelihood of a later pregnancy ending prematurely.

Rhogam: Every woman's blood should be tested for the Rh factor prior to her abortion. A woman whose blood is Rh negative may be carrying a fetus with Rh positive blood. If this is the case, within 72 hours of the abortion the woman must be given a Rhogam shot which prevents antibodies from forming which would harm a future pregnancy if that fetus was also Rh positive. The cost of Rhogam is about $40.

There are two conditions that, though rare, you should be on the lookout for. These are incomplete abortion, and more rarely, ectopic pregnancy.

Incomplete Abortion: It is possible that an abortion may be incomplete. This means a portion of the uterine contents has been missed, and the pregnancy either continues (although most likely damaged) or the remaining tissue will begin to cause an infection. Signs to look out for are an odd, musty "foul" smell from the vagina, heavy cramping, discharge, or fever. Any reputable doctor or clinic will perform a second abortion free of charge if the first one proves incomplete. It is not uncommon for incomplete abortions to occur, so be watchful and if you notice any of the above signs, call your doctor or clinic immediately.

Ectopic Pregnancy: An ectopic pregnancy is one in which the ovum has implanted in the fallopian tube, rather than in the uterus. Ectopic pregnancies are rare and are most frequently found in women with histories of pelvic inflammatory disease or scarring of the fallopian tubes. Since a fallopian tube cannot accommodate pregnancy, the conceptus will soon grow large enough to rupture the tube and cause severe internal bleeding, and possibly death.

Obviously, if you have an abortion, only the contents of the uterus are aborted and an ectopic pregnancy will remain intact. If signs of pregnancy persist after an abortion, be sure to see the doctor *immediately.*

Choosing a Facility: The following guidelines can help you choose the best possible facility for your abortion.

1. The doctor who performs the abortion should have a good medical reputation and be skilled in the method you need. It is reassuring to know that a particular doctor is well-liked by the women whom she or he has served.

2. An abortion clinic should be licensed with the state department of health and operated on a non-profit basis. The most supportive clinics are those operated by feminist health collectives. Planned Parenthood and private doctors also provide good abortion services in a clinic setting. Beware of profiteering groups which are in the "abortion business." Health care in hospital outpatient clinics can usually be trusted although the attitudes of hospital personnel vary. Check for backup services. Access to a laboratory for tests is essential. Emergency equipment, and arrangements with ambulance and nearby hospital services are important in case of an emergency. The facility should be clean and hopefully cheerful.

3. The role of an abortion counselor is to provide knowledge to a woman concerning various abortion procedures, aftercare, and birth control as well as to offer emotional support. A woman counselor should be a well-paid and well-respected member of the facility's professional team. Be sure the counselor and doctor will be supportive of you if you change your mind at the last minute. You should be encouraged but not forced to share any of your emotional feelings concerning the abortion. A good counselor is able to adapt to the needs of each woman. The presence of a counselor adds dignity and emotional support to the experience, since she is there to inform and prepare you for a procedure which someone else will be performing on you. Knowing what to expect dissolves the feeling of helplessness, which can arise during any procedure which we do not fully understand. If the only available facility does not offer counseling, you may suggest that they do so in the future. You may want to contact a feminist health collective to ask if a "patient advocate" can accompany you, especially if you feel uncomfortable about the facility. However, listen to your feelings if they tell you there is reason to feel uncomfortable. If you are really uncomfortable with the facility, you should do your best to find another one.

4. Be sure the procedure suggested is the best for the length of your pregnancy. Ask if the doctor will be using a flexible rather than a non-flexible cannula if you are having a vacuum abortion.

Be sure all instruments are sterilized for each patient.

5. It is helpful to ask the following questions: Are post-abortion Rhogam shots given if necessary? Is a recovery room provided? Will you receive written results of the pathology tests done on the fetal tissue? Is local anaesthesia given for first trimester abortions? Will copies of your medical records be made available upon request? Does the facility require payment in advance? (It is better to pay on the day of your appointment in case you change you mind.) Are health insurance and Medicaid accepted? A woman may often qualify for emergency medical assistance to pay for her abortion. Minors may confidentially apply for medical assistance irrespective of their parents' income in California. Other states may operate differently. Be sure the fees are fair.

6. No facility has the right to maintain any consent regulations which request that a woman obtain permission from her husband or parents for the abortion. If such regulations exist you can take legal action, but first have your own need taken care of by going elsewhere, if possible.

CHAPTER FOUR

Alternatives to Abortion

Life is full of choices. We have to consider alternatives, bene-
fits, and disadvantages and decide. We can't do everything.
                                    Dr. Elizabeth M. Whelan, Sc.D.

NOW THAT ABORTION IS A LEGAL OPTION, more women are making
the choice to terminate an unplanned pregnancy. There are still
many women, however, who do not feel that abortion is the best
solution for them. There are two constructive alternatives to abortion: one is continuing the pregnancy and giving the baby up for
adoption, the second is continuing the pregnancy and preparing
oneself to meet the unexpected demands of childrearing. Deciding
to continue your pregnancy and continuing to regard it as unwanted is not a constructive alternative. There is growing evidence
to suggest a woman's attitude toward her growing fetus is communicated. It is extremely important, then, that very early in a
woman's pregnancy she decides exactly what course of action she
will take.

Adoption: If a woman knows she will be giving her baby up for
adoption it is still important that she accept herself throughout her
pregnancy, and this also means having an attitude of acceptance
towards the fetus. Wanting to give birth to a child and making arrangements for the baby to be raised by adoptive parents who will
love her or him is providing for the well-being of that child. Luck-
ily, children are being placed in adoptive homes much more quickly than ever before. Of course, healthy babies find homes much

more readily than unhealthy babies, which is another very good reason for accepting the pregnancy and being good to yourself thoughout it. How well you take care of yourself during your pregnancy (diet, exercise, medical care, emotional environment) will affect your baby's health.

The adoption process includes signing over all your legal rights and responsibilities as parent of your child to an unknown person described to you by an agency. Once the final papers are signed, the decision is irreversible.

Only the natural mother, no matter what her age or financial status, can legally give a baby up for adoption. Even if others try to influence your decision, you are the only one who can actually decide. No one can take your baby away from you. This includes your parents and the father of the child. The only rare exception is if a woman is proven to be mentally incompetent, which is generally very difficult to prove legally. You should be aware, however, that *if* you name a father on the birth certificate, he must give his consent for the adoption. You do have the option of *not* naming the father.

If you are legally married, your husband must give his consent in order for you to give up the baby for adoption. This is true even if you are married and the father of the child is not your husband, if you have not seen your husband for years, or if divorce proceedings were finalized less than three hundred days before. If you are in any of these situations, you should consult a lawyer immediately. If you cannot afford a private lawyer, consult your local Legal Aid society.

There are two kinds of adoption—agency adoption and independent or private adoption. Adoption agencies are sometimes part of the state Department of Social Welfare. Some are independent and non-sectarian like the Children's Home Society in California. Many others are privately administered by religious organizations. Adoption practices vary from agency to agency.

As soon as you decide to continue your pregnancy, even if you are not absolutely sure you want to give the baby up for adoption, it is very important to contact the adoption agencies in your area and explore the procedure. You can always change your mind, since final adoption papers cannot be signed until after the child is born, but you cannot always have your baby placed immediately in a permanent home if you delay. It is important for you to have the adoption proceedings underway if there is any chance at all that adoption will be your final choice.

If you choose to go through an agency, which is generally the most hassle-free for the mother, the first step is to contact an agency and make an appointment with a social worker. This initial appointment will be made only if the agency is confident it can place your baby. If one agency's quota has been met, then try another. Over the next few months the social worker will meet with you a few times to gather information on the baby's background. This helps the agency place the baby in the most appropriate home. The adoption proceedings will be explained during these interviews and you should feel free to ask any questions you have. *Applying to an adoption agency does not put you under obligation to give the baby away.* Even after the baby is born, should you decide to keep her or him, the adoption worker can usually refer you to appropriate agencies offering assistance in childrearing.

Most agencies ask that final adoption papers be signed between two and six weeks after the baby is born. Although the agency will arrange for the baby to be taken from the hospital and placed in a temporary home until the mother decides, the child is never placed in its permanent home until the legal proceedings are final. It is much better for the child to be placed in a permanent home as quickly as possible. Adoptive parents are rigorously screened to be sure they will be good parents. Many of the proceedings are so demanding that people who could make very good parents either do not meet all the requirements or do not care to submit to the screening process. The Adoption Resource Exchange of North America has been established to help people who want to adopt children get in touch with those who want to give their children up for adoption. Some babies are "hard-to-place" because of racially mixed backgrounds or health problems. The Exchange is particularly helpful in these situations.

Agencies protect both the natural mother and adoptive parents from knowing details of each others lives. Only general information is given to each about the other. The baby will receive a new birth certificate with the adoptive parents listed. The original birth certificate is kept in the agency's vault. The adoptive parents, rather than the natural mother, pay the agency's fee.

Adopted children are very much wanted by their parents. There is a lot of red tape a couple must go through to qualify to have a child placed with them. Because of the financial and emotional commitment and the waiting involved, adoptive parents are obviously interested in providing a good life for their child. Many adopted children feel very "special" because they know they were really wanted. There is a natural curiosity about their natural parents, but most children who were adopted consider their true parents those that nurtured them through their childhood years. Some adopted children, however, do grow up with the feeling that their natural parents rejected them. These children may later need counseling and professional help in understanding and accepting their adoptive status.

Independent adoption occurs when the natural mother gets in touch with adopting parents without help of an agency. Complications can arise when trying to make arrangements yourself and having no other alternative open can leave the natural mother without a home in which to place her child. In an independent adoption, anytime prior to the signing of legal adoption papers, either the natural mother or the adopting parents can change their minds; even after the baby is placed in their home. The state Department of Social Welfare must still approve a couple for adoption before the papers can be signed, but the criteria are more relaxed than those of an agency. It is good to select a lawyer who has experience in this field to prepare the papers for you.

Sometimes a woman chooses a member of her own family to adopt her child. The advantage to this is being able to watch your child grow and the disadvantage is pretending you are not the child's mother and possibly having to explain to the child why you chose not to take care of her or him.

Giving a child up for adoption naturally involves a sense of loss. For nine months a woman's body and mind are involved in pregnancy and suddenly the pregnancy is over and the child is gone. Feeling depressed after giving a child away is very understandable, yet the degree of depression is different for each individual. A sense of loss can co-exist with a strong acceptance of one's choice. You will need all of your energy to continue your own life and perhaps make a lot of new beginnings. If you are experiencing depression, loss, or sadness, some of the anecdotes mentioned in Chapter Five may help. You might also consider seeking professional counseling if your feelings persist.

One woman who gave her child away expressed her feelings in these words:

> After carrying Magdelena for nine months it is very painful to let her go now that I can see her and touch her. And yet I know I would not be a good mother for her now. Deeper than all my pain, though, is the joy that giving birth has brought me. I feel important because I am Magdelena's mother and so grateful that she has taught me that true love means letting go.[21]

If you are considering adoption, there are many other questions you are probably wondering about, such as: Do I tell my family and friends or do I disappear for six months? How do I support myself while I'm pregnant? How do I get medical care? Will I qualify for assistance if I move to another state? All these considerations are outside the scope of this book, but are very well answered by Ruth I. Pierce in her book *Single and Pregnant* published by Beacon Press.

Many teenage women who choose to give their babies up for adoption also choose to live in a maternity home during their pregnancies, I will discuss this topic in Chapter Seven.

Single Parenting: More women than ever before are accepting the challenge of single parenting. In some areas, being a single mother is well-accepted. There are many good books which describe the joys and difficulties of single parenting. One of these is *Momma Handbook: The Sourcebook for Single Mothers*, edited by Karol Hope and Nancy Young. Another is *Creative Survival for Single Mothers*, written by Persia Woolley and published by Celestial Arts, in which she says:

> Being a single mother is not the end of the world after all, and with a little thoughtful planning and a fair sense of humor you can achieve a pretty full life, but it does take some doing.[22]

It is very wise to talk to single mothers before deciding to become one yourself. Once the decision is clear, you might even choose to move to an area of the country where you can receive emotional support and acceptance from the community at large as well as from the growing community of single mothers.

Even if a woman clearly does not want to maintain a primary relationship with the father of her child, it is often possible to work out an agreement with him whereby he accepts partial responsibility for childrearing. This arrangement should be made before the birth of the child, but it should not become a major factor in deciding to be a single mother. It is much easier on a woman in the long run if she regards her responsibility to the child as the primary factor when deciding whether or not she is willing to go it alone.

Before you decide on single parenting, it would be a good idea to take some time to look at the hard realities of single parenting. Many women have a romanticized idea of parenthood and feel "everything will work out." Get a pencil and paper and figure out whether or not you can financially support a child. How will you pay the hospital and doctor fees? (Medicaid may pay for some of this.) Can you afford food, clothing, medical bills for a child? Can you afford childcare? Where will you leave the child while you are working? Are you ready to cope with the demands a baby will place on your time? Are you ready to make a long-term commitment? Are you prepared for the change a child will bring to your personal and social life?

Women are beginning to rely more on each other for help in childrearing. Single mothers are forming play groups and day care centers which nurture their children as well as free themselves to pursue other activities. Some women are even joining together to form communities in which childrearing becomes a collective effort. If the responsibilities of each member of the group are defined and the time schedules can be coordinated, this method of easing the burden of single motherhood can be a source of great joy and growth for mothers and children alike.

Raising a child alone does not preclude the possibility of forming a fulfilling relationship with a man who accepts and loves your child and enjoys assuming the fathering role. There are many reasons for a woman's choice to raise a child alone. Although most women would prefer to raise a child within a healthy relationship with a man, circumstances sometimes prevent this. Pregnancy may interfere with the ripening of a love relationship or may occur despite the fact that the relationship itself was withering, or there may have been no real relationship to begin with. A woman who is nearing the end of her childbearing years may opt to become a single parent rather than miss the opportunity for motherhood.

In order to grow, a single mother needs to be aware of her own needs for companionship and stimulation. The tendency to make a child the center of your universe is not particularly healthy for you or the child. Children thrive on contact with other children and adults; mothers, single and otherwise, need a fulfilled life like everyone else. If you feel you cannot fulfill your own needs as well as those of a child, it would be wise to reject the idea of single parenting.

The Farm: A creative and loving alternative to abortion is The Farm, a community of 650 people, 200 of them children, in Tennessee. Any woman who is pregnant and feels unable to care for the coming child by herself is welcome to come to this community and deliver her baby with the help of their highly competent and compassionate midwives (or local doctors if necessary). She may then leave the baby in the care of one of the families and is free to return at any time in the future and reclaim her child. The mother's visit on the land, her birthing, and the care of the child are all freely given as a gift of love. The community is founded on the universal principles of love, joy, and honesty, which are found in every religion. Steve Gaskin, author of *The Caravan* and *Monday Night Class* is considered a teacher by the members of The Farm. Gaskin and the members of The Farm wrote about their community achievements in *The Farm Book.*

A pregnant mother who comes to The Farm for help sometimes becomes a member of the community, or may be strengthened through the love and support they receive and leave The Farm with (or without) the child. Women interested in this alternative should investigate it thoroughly, since distance, relocation, philosophy, and other factors must be taken into account.

Making Room For One More: Over 50 percent of unplanned pregnancies occur to single or married women with families of one or more children. Even within a happy marriage most couples want and need to limit the size of their families. Couples often agree that they have the time, energy, and finances for a certain number of children and no more. It is important to take into account your own individual limitations.

If you decide to continue this pregnancy and make preparations to rearrange your life to include an unexpected addition to your family, chances are you do not want to face this situation again. Be sure to read the chapter on prevention. Women who come from certain cultural backgrounds may find it difficult to limit their families because of pressure from husbands, relatives, or cultural beliefs. If you want to make this pregnancy your last it will be helpful to face these pressures and begin to assert what *you* want in life even if it is not future motherhood.

Resources: Many of the factors which determine a woman's choice to adopt or keep her child depend on her inner feelings as well as the outer circumstances of her life. No matter which you choose it is important to be well-housed, fed, medically cared for, and emotionally nourished during your pregnancy. Dealing with agencies isn't always easy or enjoyable. Some personnel are not particularly kind either due to their work load, their own problems, or their attitude toward those seeking help. You have a right to the necessities of life and you have the right to be treated with respect. If you have trouble with someone in an agency, I suggest you ask to see that person's supervisor. Acting with self-respect and self-assertion will help to bring you the respect and the resources you need. If you have a hard time dealing with bureaucracies and people in authority, especially when you feel vulnerable, it might be helpful to read one of the books on Assertiveness Training. See Suggested Reading for further information.

If you are single or married, pregnant, or feel the burden of too many children already, the following agencies can be helpful in meeting your various needs:

Department of Social Welfare
Maternity and Infant Care Projects
Maternity Homes
Family Service Agencies (Jewish, Lutheran, Catholic)
United Community Service Bureau
Free Clinics
Local Switchboards
Red Cross
Youth Emergency Services
International Service Agency
Travelers Aid
Ministers, Priests, Rabbis
College Counselors
Local Unified School District (to continue studies while home)
YWCA
Florence Crittenton Home for Unwed Mothers

Changing Circumstances: A woman may know she would want to continue her pregnancy if some of the external circumstances could be changed. There are ways to obtain financial assistance and ways to raise children creatively so that a woman can continue her education or career (at least part-time). One circumstance a woman often has no power over is the attitude of the man with whom she conceived. Perhaps the man has offered to marry you for the sake of the future child. Such marriages do not have a very high success rate. A marriage can be happy if it has been precipitated by an unplanned pregnancy, but usually only if love and care already existed, and the couple wanted to get married anyway. Even so, the going is rough at first. Marriage is never the answer to all of a person's problems. It is a challenge in and of itself, with and without children.

Destructive Alternative—The Unwanted Child: Continuing an unwanted pregnancy and ultimately bearing an unwanted child which a woman keeps but resents is *no* alternative to anything. It is self-destructive and unfair to the child. Poor women in conservative states still have difficulties obtaining abortions.

What effect does a woman being forced to bear (or intentionally bearing) her unwanted child have upon the child itself? Professor Hardin, a well-known writer on abortion also asks that question.

> Is it good that a woman who does not want a child should bear one? As abundant literature in psychology and sociology proves, the unwanted child is a social danger. Unwanted children are more likely than others to become delinquents, and . . . when they become parents themselves may breed another generation of unwanted children. This is a vicious circle if ever there was one . . . In this day of the population explosion, society has no reason to encourage the birth of more children; but it has a tremendous interest in encouraging the birth of more wanted children.[23]

There are 300,000 children in foster homes at any given time in our country. Drs. Steel and Pollack, authors of the *Battered Child*, force us to look closely at a few children's lives out of the 50,000 that are severely battered or killed each year. Even if a parent has never physically expressed her or his resentment toward an unwanted child, the unconscious message is communicated to the child. In Erich Neuman's book, *The Child*, he tells us that the primal relationship is the foundation of all subsequent relationships. Therefore, the quality of the mother-child relationship has far-reaching consequences.

Beyond Motherhood: Facing the crises of an unplanned pregnancy creates awareness as to our roles as mothers, and beyond this, as women in society. Only in the last forty years has it been possible for women to plan to avoid unwanted pregnancies and to organize their lives on this basis. Many women are choosing to limit the size of their families, delay childbearing, and remain childless. Women are beginning to view the actualization of their own potential as valuable and as a complement to childrearing. Each woman suddenly has many choices which were not available to her previously. If childrearing is no longer inevitable, then a woman must look beyond the maternal role for meaning and fulfillment in life. Many women have been "cultured" to be mothers from their earliest years. For them it is especially difficult to unlearn old habits of thinking and begin to explore new ways of "being in the world." Some women find that childrearing is very compatible with their own growth.

The possible childrearing arrangements are only limited by our own creativity. Having children and developing one's own life is no longer an either/or proposition.

The nuclear family is opening up to embrace friends, neighbors, and relatives. The extended family is being revived. Women are inviting their men to participate in childrearing while they themselves take more responsibility for the economic needs of the family. The women's movement has resulted in a new love and appreciation between individual women, so that caring for each other's children becomes a concrete expression of support. Parents are organizing play groups and children's centers which, when properly supplied and staffed, are more beneficial to a child's intellectual and emotional development than the constant isolation of her or his own home. Nursery schools accept children sometimes as young as 1½ years old now, allowing parents more free time, yet offer a mother the opportunity to contribute a limited number of hours to participate in the school environment; in this way, mothers can learn and grow with their children, and at the same time, come into contact with various views on childraising through their participation. Children are becoming part of life again and are not being separated from their parents and from other children as they have been since the industrial revolution. Parents are taking their kids backpacking, to movies, and on long trips.

The difficulties of raising children can be diminished by learning some essentials from parent training classes, nursery school co-ops, or from reading some practical guides to parenting.

The quantity of time a woman spends with her child is never as important as the quality of that time. Setting aside time each day to do an activity with the child or simply to talk, creates a special bond and a feeling of being loved on the part of the child. Children can learn to respect their mothers' time alone and can become more autonomous in developing their own interests if a mother communicates that need to her child in a non-rejecting way. Stating the way it is, and following through by taking time for yourself is of utmost importance. This is called "setting limits."

Some women choose professions which require extensive and uninterrupted training to gain proficiency and/or licensing. To have a child midway in the educational process could result in a severe setback. Bearing children when a woman definitely wants them and has room for them in her life serves the best interest of both mother and child. Bearing children later in life allows a woman to bring an added maturity to her experience. The more fulfilled we are the more we have to give another. A healthy life-style has more influence on the ease of childbearing and the well-being of the child than the age of the mother. Many women thirty to forty are bearing their first child with ease and the joy that can only come from free choice, good physical health, and emotional maturity.

Reaching the end of the childbearing years still childless raises the question, "Now? or never?" Perhaps a woman's circumstances are not ideal. Then there is the question, "Will there ever be a time any better?" Time is short. What do you do? Each woman must decide for herself and this is no easy decision. If one feels a link between one's identity as a woman and childbearing, it is important not to allow that feeling to be a major factor in decision-making. The reason to have a child should not be primarily egocentric, but rather what one can offer another human being. The actual decision to never have children can be put off for many years. But once the physical deadline has been reached, it is important a woman reaches a psychological closure for herself on the issue. There is no need for regrets.

Answering the following questions may help you clarify some of your thoughts in regard to children. There may be still other questions and alternatives you may think of yourself. I hope to at least have stimulated your thinking on the subject.

1. Am I finished with my schooling and/or professional training?
2. Will it be difficult to resume my schooling/training if I take time out for childbearing and the early years of child-rearing?
3. How much time do I want to spend in childrearing?
4. With whom can I share the responsibility of childrearing?
5. Am I financially independent? How can I work and raise a child?
6. Can I relate well with children? Do I enjoy children?
7. What can I offer a child in terms of my capacities as a mother?
8. What are my real motivations in wanting to have children?
9. Do I resent unforeseen interruptions in my daily schedule?
10. Is anyone pressuring me to have this child?
11. Is anyone pressuring me to give this child up for adoption?
12. What do I want?

Chapter Five offers some other suggestions which can be helpful in deciding whether you want to keep the child or give it up for adoption.

PRO-LIFE

Right to Life and Birthright are two pro-life organizations devoted to the continuation of pregnancy. Both these groups are distinctly anti-abortion and do not consider abortion an alternative to *anything* or feel a choice is even involved—the only "choice" is to continue the pregnancy. A woman seeking assistance from one of these organizations will be urged very strongly to continue her pregnancy, and therefore must be very sure this will be her final choice before contacting either organization. For a woman who *is* *sure* she wants to continue her pregnancy, these organizations can be extremely helpful.

Right to Life is a slogan used by persons involved in a political movement to repeal the existing abortion law or at least make it difficult for this law to function. This group obviously does not feel a woman has the right to choose an abortion, and is in favor of enforcing pregnancy by law. The basis for their fervent activities is the belief that the "moment" of conception marks the beginning of personhood and that every fetus has the right to be born. One organization which upholds the Right to Life philosophy but claims no political involvement in anti-abortion activities is Birthright.

Birthright: In response to the legalization of abortion in the United States, a Toronto housewife, Louise Summerhill, formed Birthright. This organization believes that every woman has the right (obligation) to give birth and every fetus has the right to be born. Birthright operates mainly through the efforts of volunteers who answer phone calls from, and meet with, women who have problem pregnancies. This organization does serve the real need of helping women (especially young ones) who want to continue their pregnancies but who are having difficulties such as low finances, inadequate housing, and no emotional support. *All* young women are encouraged to continue their pregnancies no matter what their problems may be. In this respect, Birthright can be a helpful service for those who are *sure* they want to continue their pregnancies.

However, Birthright includes in its charter a moral denouncement of abortion. Any woman who seeks this agency's help, therefore, will not be encouraged to choose anything but continuing her pregnancy. The Birthright people have adopted biased attitudes and questionable facts which can easily influence a woman who is ambivalent about her pregnancy. A woman who is uncertain as to what she wants to do about an unplanned pregnancy can be just as easily pushed into carrying her pregnancy to term as easily as into an abortion. Neither of these should happen. Deciding whether to have an abortion or have the child should be done on the basis of true, objective facts and should take into account the individual needs, feelings, and attitudes of the woman choosing. Below are cited statements from Louise Summerhill's book, *Birthright,* which through my research I have discovered to be totally unfounded and erroneous. Following each paraphrased statement, I have written a response (marked *R.*) in which I have attempted to give the facts as they appear in reputable sources.

1. Abortion is very dangerous, the mortality rate is high.

R. This statement is far more valid for illegal abortions. When abortions were illegal, it was estimated that 10,000 women died each year through obtaining illegal abortions. The New York City Health Services Administration Report of December 6, 1973, states that in New York City the 1972–73 mortality rate was 2 per 100,000 abortions. During 1970–73 the maternal mortality rate was 38.3 per 100,000 live births.[24] The mortality rate for abortions that are *legal*, therefore, was much lower than the mortality rate for childbirth. Only illegal abortions are "very dangerous."

2. Risk of sterility in teenagers is 33⅓ percent.

R. Studies show that the risk of sterility ranges between 1 to 27.7 percent with most studies in the 3 percent range.

3. The fetus has already developed a heartbeat three weeks after conception.

R. The fetal heart does not develop to the point of beating until 20 weeks LMP. (A good resource for fetal development is Geraldine Flanagan's *The First Nine Months of Life*.)

4. Abortion causes psychological damage, inescapable regrets and intolerable guilt.

R. One of the most complete studies done on this subject is quoted on page 107. The results indicate that the overwhelming majority of women (75 percent) suffer no self-reproaches following abortion, and the remainder who did felt they were somehow pressured into the choice to abort. Therefore, *a woman's own attitude is the most important factor in the psychological impact of abortion.* Judith Wallerstein in an article, "Psychosocial Sequelae of Therapeutic Abortion in Young Unmarried Women," states that in six-month and one-year followup studies, most women had used their abortion experience as a creative one which helped build ego strength.[25]

5. Extramarital sex is not moral, but since we are all sinners, the unmarried pregnant woman should be treated with love and compassion and she will, thereby, naturally realize the error of her ways.

R. Many studies show that the very idea that sex is not moral leads to unwanted pregnancies through a woman's lack of accepting responsibility for her own sexuality and not using birth control. One such study is discussed in detail in Kristin Luker's *Taking Chances*.[26] No information on contraceptives is given to a woman, even if she has the courage to ask for it.

6. The pro-abortion climate of society pushes women into accepting abortion as the only way out of an unwanted pregnancy.

R. Before abortion was legalized, an estimated 1,000,000 abortions were performed each year in a very anti-abortion climate. Now a woman is legally free to choose abortion, and in 1974 approximately 1,000,000 such operations were performed. Granted, now that abortion is legal, society in general is exhibiting a more accepting attitude. When women have the right to choose whether or not to continue a pregnancy, their health and lives are protected but the number of women choosing abortions does not significantly increase.

7. There is really no population problem. There need be no limit to the number of children we can welcome into the world. Large families are natural.

R. The rate of population growth is increasing rapidly (by 70 million per year). Overpopulation is a concept that can be misunderstood and manipulated. Basically, overpopulation means that the amount of resources necessary to human life are not adequate to serve the numbers of people. Presently, half of the world's population is undernourished. We would have to double our present production of food in order to feed the people we have right now—let alone those we will have next year, and the year after.[27] We do need more people to use their full capacity for creative and intelligent thinking to find solutions to these problems. In the interim, however, mindless reproduction will only increase the numbers of humans suffering. Natural life is a fulfilled life. For that, we need to attend to the quality of life and responsibly control our human fertility.

8. Womanly virtue rests in motherhood. Those who have abortions are unwomanly.

R. Many, many women who are not mothers feel very affirmed in their womanliness. Among such women are artist Judy Chicago, writer Anais Nin, dancer Martha Graham (and many more), all of whom have created beautiful and inspirational expressions through their womanliness. A woman can be a mother but being a woman includes so much more.

9. Illegal abortions continue despite the new law.

R. In Los Angeles County, the University of Southern California Medical Center noted that, following the 1967 liberalization of California's abortion law, the number of women treated for clandestine abortions dropped from 800 to 100 per year, and this law was still somewhat restrictive (requiring that women get a letter from a psychiatrist to verify that the pregnancy was a threat to her mental health). No woman would take recourse to an illegal abortion when a medically safe abortion was readily available.[28]

10. No benefits are ever mentioned for legalizing abortion, with ample evidence that abortion continues, whether legal or not.
R. The approximate mortality rate for illegal abortions is 20.8 per 100,000. In New York City between 1972 and 1973, it was found that the mortality rate dropped to 2 deaths per 100,000 following the liberalization of the abortion law.[29] This is one tenth the death rate as for illegal abortions. Obviously, legalization of abortion benefits women having abortions. The reduction in unwanted children benefits society as a whole. This point is elaborated in the last chapter.

11. As long as there are couples who want to adopt babies then we cannot "really say babies are unwanted."
R. Despite the difficulty in adopting a white normal baby there are many other children who are older, of other races, or children with exceptional problems who are now being adopted that were not before. There are still 300,000 children in foster homes in our country at any one time. Certainly no woman should be forced into continuing her pregnancy so that those who cannot have children of their own may adopt. Even if a woman may be assured of giving her child to good adoptive parents, she may not want to go through with her pregnancy.

There is a difference between holding an opinion about abortion based on personal belief, and presenting information on abortion which is simply untrue. If a person's or agency's position is based on dishonest information, it is easy to doubt the motivation involved. In the years prior to the legalization of abortion, women were in even greater need of a service such as Birthright. No one seemed to care that hundreds of thousands of women were suffering from the real dangers of illegal abortions. Now that abortion is safe and legal, Birthright has emerged. In everything Birthright says and does there is an implied set of moral values: sex outside marriage is not moral; although forgivable, all conceptions should be carried through to term, and a person exists from conception onwards.

12. Finally the creed of Birthright as composed by Louise Summerhill:

> To uphold, at all times, that any pregnant girl or woman has the right to whatever help she may need to carry her child to term, and to foster respect for human life at all stages of development.[30]

R. If Birthright stayed within the context of that creed it would indeed be performing a noble service. However, when counseling tactics and advertisements based on unfounded information are designed to convince a woman that abortion is morally wrong, "Do you realize that your baby's heart was beating three weeks after conception and that he is a human being who someday may thank you for the gift of life?" and that abortion is very dangerous, "The truth is that if you have an abortion and survive the dangers of blood poisoning, embolism or excessive bleeding you could be sterilized and the child you now carry would then be your only one," it is obvious that Birthright does not respect a woman's right to choose what she wants to do about an unplanned pregnancy. In fact, the risks of childbearing for a young teenage woman are three times as great than the risks of abortion. The psychological consequences of giving up a child for adoption are far more upsetting than having an abortion. If an agency, supposedly devoted to helping women, engages in the practice of presenting false information and applying psychological pressure on women to make the only decision Birthright wants them to make, then it is obvious that Birthright is not set up to truly help women, but only to espouse their own credo.

We see the world through our belief systems, through the values we assign to different events. We are living in a time of social transition. Old restrictive moral codes are giving way to new standards of health and fulfillment. Guilt and punishment are being replaced by a faith in the natural tendency of life to grow towards wholeness. We are beginning to understand that respect for various cultures and religions does not threaten our capacity to live according to our own chosen values. The responsibility for making major life decisions rests no longer with the group, but with the individual. We are faced with the awesome challenge to create our lives according to our own personal vision. Making choices about concrete issues such as which profession to enter, where to settle, who to choose for friends, or whether or not to marry and if so, whom, are often accompanied by anxiety even though no moral issue is attached. It is clear that anxiety accompanies any choice of importance.

Only the woman who unquestioningly accepts the view that abortion is a forbidden act, need not make a personal choice regarding her unplanned pregnancy. She does, however, have to choose to keep the child or give it up for adoption, and rearrange her life accordingly. For most women, an unplanned pregnancy presents them with the demand to choose either to continue that pregnancy or to terminate it.

What are the questions women might ask themselves in the process of deciding?

- When do I believe that the fetus becomes a person?
- If the contents of my uterus are not yet a human person, but only the potential for a human person then is it acceptable to me to terminate my pregnancy and, if so, what are my reasons?
- If I believe that the contents of my uterus is now a human person, can I accept, within myself, terminating this pregnancy?
- How will this pregnancy affect my own health, my self-concept, the quality of my life, my feelings about myself as a woman? How will it affect my relationships with significant others, my economic status, professional commitments, or the time and energy already being spent in childrearing?
- What is the value of continuing or terminating this pregnancy for my own self-development?
- If this pregnancy were continued, what would be the quality of life I could offer the child that would be born?

CHAPTER FIVE

Attitudes
and Antidotes

From sharing our personal struggles we can recognize what
we need to heal in ourselves and what needs to be healed in
our culture.

Anica Vesel Mander/Anne Kent Rush

IT IS COMMON KNOWLEDGE AMONG WOMEN that many of us do not
use birth control properly or at all. Among professionals who work
with women seeking abortions, this phenomenon elicits more
anger, disrespect, and lack of understanding than any other.
Women of all ages, socioeconomic backgrounds, and educational
levels have neglected to use birth control at one time or other. How
can women be so irresponsible, they wonder? The answer lies, in
part, with certain attitudes which can be faced and transcended—
if we only learn how.

If you are now pregnant because you did not use birth control,
stop here and answer the following questions. This may help you
understand your own attitudes and feelings that may have contributed to your becoming pregnant.

- Did I fully understand how conception occurs?
- Did I think I couldn't get pregnant?
- Did I try to get birth control and was refused?
- Do I feel okay about having sex?
- Do I feel that using birth control makes sex less spontaneous?
- Did I want to become pregnant, but it didn't work out the way I
  thought it would? Did I do it to push him into marrying me?

- Do I want to have a child in the future, but didn't realize that until now?
- What does "having a baby" mean for me?
- What does "being a mother" mean to me?
- Did I want to have something of my own—something that only belongs to me?
- Am I trying to show my independence?

There are certain common attitudes which influence risking an unwanted pregnancy. The first part of this chapter will examine these and the second part will explore how it is possible for women to grow beyond them.

DANGEROUS ATTITUDES

Ignorance Born of Doubt and Fear: Non-use or incorrect use of birth control often stems from lack of knowledge. It is very important to have a clear understanding of our body's reproductive power. Often such knowledge is not routinely taught in schools. Although many high schools now offer sex education as part of a health class, birth control information may not be part of the course.

Many young women are afraid their parents will find out if they go to a local Planned Parenthood office. Asking the family doctor about such matters is often unthinkable, because it is assumed the doctor will tell the family, as some well might. Older sisters, especially married ones it is felt "won't understand." This fear of "being discovered" or "found out" is a sure breeding ground for doubt and misinformation. Even the most sheltered teenagers have heard or read something about birth control. That little bit of knowledge can lead to very high-risk sexual activity. Many popular myths about conception are the topics of discussion in high-school locker rooms.

Continuing to participate in sexual activity while harboring fears and doubts concerning effective protection from pregnancy is irresponsible. Responsible sexual behavior includes the conscious knowledge of the possible consequences of sexual intercourse—one being pregnancy—and taking measures to prevent this from occurring. If fears and doubts are strong enough, they can restrict a woman's view of her sexual activity so that she allows herself to be very passive in her sexual role. This can be true for a woman of any age. To admit that she wants regular sexual intercourse may be too anxiety-producing, especially if she comes from a social or religious background which disapproves of sex outside marriage. Taking responsibility for her sexual desires by protecting herself with birth control is to consciously set herself against the mores and morals of her family, and perhaps even her friends. A woman caught in such a dilemma may express her sexual experiences as "happening" to her, rather than as an event in which she participates.

How can a woman prevent these attitudes of doubt and fear from overcoming her common sense? Sexual feelings and desires for sexual intimacy are normal, natural human experiences. Often the stirrings of these sexual feelings are strong and exciting when we least expect it. The sexual excitement is pleasurable, but if a woman is taught these feelings are bad, she is left with a contradiction to somehow reconcile. Millions of women are beginning to admit their desire for a satisfying sex life for the first time. Too often, women have accepted the taboo against enjoying sexuality. Just reading that other women are in the same situation doesn't help much. Talking with friends can ease the loneliness somewhat, but usually doesn't help with the confusion. A Woman's Center is an excellent place to go to talk to other women about sexual feelings, fears, doubts, to ask about birth control, and to learn about our bodies. See the bibliography for references.

Lack of Self-Respect: If a woman does not respect herself, she may allow her health to suffer through improper diet or lack of exercise, keep herself stuck in a poisonous environment, or fail to protect herself from an unwanted pregnancy. If you have been suffering from feelings of inferiority lately, (the "I'm not good enough" syndrome), it's a warning signal to be careful. Feelings of self-negation usually lie deep within the psyche. To "act out" and become pregnant on the basis of these feelings only compounds the problem. Some women have used "getting pregnant" as a form of self-punishment, or as a way to give themselves something of their own in order to feel more valuable as a person. "I don't care what happens to me," is the expression often used by women who are caught in this trap; or "I thought I would be valued more as a woman if I produced a child."

How do you get out of this? A woman who lacks respect for herself needs help. If her feelings strongly interfere with her life, she may benefit most from seeing a private counselor. Often, a feminist therapist can most easily help a woman affirm herself and let go of self-destructive patterns. If her feelings about herself affect her very deeply, a consciousness-raising group can help her clarify her feelings, gain support for change, and grow toward more positive behavior. Consciousness-raising groups mainly provide empathy and support for change, rather than trying to uncover reasons rooted in childhood for a person's problem.

Loneliness: We women have the potential to create a new person, a child who is completely dependent on us for food, shelter, love, and protection for the beginning years of her or his life. If we are feeling lonely or unfulfilled in our relationships, it may become a temptation, often an unconscious one, to have a child in order to fill our need to love and be loved. If a woman brings a child into the world with the intention of fulfilling her own need for companionship, she will probably smother that child with overconcern and overindulgence. It is healthier to reach out to other adults in order to move away from self-induced isolation. If we can't enjoy the friendship of independent adults, it may be even more difficult to enjoy the total dependency of a child. If we are feeling needy, how can we give to a child? We can only give from our own fullness. It is our responsibility to create a joyous environment for a child, from within ourselves—not bring a child into our life to fulfill us.

Karma: In some groups we often hear the word "karma" given as an explanation for events, especially very good or very bad ones. The general understanding of this word is that everything that happens has its roots in what has come before it, and therefore we cannot do much about changing our lives. Actually the sanskrit word simply means "action" and as modern physics is beginning to recognize, every activity in the universe stands in relationship to every other—the cosmos is a dynamic interrelated flow of energy. Laws of nature we do not understand completely are constantly at work. In the realm of birth control and pregnancy, this could apply to the unexpected pregnancies which occur using reliable methods of birth control. Why some methods do not work for some women is still somewhat of a mystery. An equally inexplicable situation is that some women use no birth control for years without becoming pregnant and then suddenly they conceive. However, the *action* of sexual intercourse without birth control is likely to result in pregnancy and that is no mystery to any of us. If we allow ourselves to remain unprotected from an unwanted pregnancy we are creating our own "karma." To take responsibility for our lives, including our capacity for childbearing, means taking an active role in preventing or preparing for pregnancy before the fact—to allow pregnancy to just "happen" is to use the concept of "karma" as an excuse for being passive and not taking responsibility.

Female Role: It has been said that one of the most popular reasons for having children is "to fulfill myself as a woman." Many women still feel motherhood is essential to their womanliness. A woman's upbringing may have prepared her for nothing else. Perhaps you do not think that mothering is the main purpose for your existence, but if it's not, then what part (if any) does mothering play in your life? Even if you are sure you want children, perhaps you still want to maintain a profession or other interests. Child-rearing and a life of one's own need not be an either/or proposition, but timing is important. Also, many women are happily opting to remain childless. Part II can give you some suggestions for clarifying what you want most and when. An excellent article which explores and negates the motherhood myth is *Motherhood, Who Needs It?* which is available from the National Organization for Non-Parents.

Growing Up: Most cultures throughout the world hold special ceremonies at important transition points in a person's life: birth, puberty, marriage, and death. Our culture has no established mode of welcoming a young woman or man into the adult community. This rite of passage from childhood to adulthood is a profoundly effective means of stabilizing the new mature status of the person for her or himself and for all the community. It sometimes happens that a woman who is struggling with her autonomy begins to view pregnancy as the only concrete way of establishing herself as a fully mature member of society. This is especially true when a young woman comes from a background in which a woman's main responsibility is considered to be raising children. Some women choose to become mothers very early in life and that may be the best choice for them. For other young women this is impractical. Being a woman involves more than being a mother. We each have important contributions to make to society born from our uniqueness as a woman and as a person. A woman's studies program can be a tremendous help in broadening our scope of possibilities.

Fertility: If a woman has never had a child or has not had one in many years, she may doubt her capacity to become pregnant. Knowing that one is fertile is important to some women but becoming pregnant and having an abortion is not the easiest way to find out. If you are becoming concerned about your fertility there are more positive ways you can learn about yourself. Taking a self-help class can give you greater knowledge and techniques with which to understand your body. You can feel yourself ovulate once you become tuned in to your own body. Some women feel a slight twinge in the area of the ovary which only lasts a few seconds. Others feel a more dramatic sensation which fills the whole pelvic region and perhaps the lower back as well. Classes in natural methods of birth control also teach such signs of ovulation as fertile mucus and temperature changes. Observance of these signs can reassure a woman she is indeed fertile. The more we understand our own bodies, the more we can enjoy experiencing the rhythms and cycles which are an integral part of our feminine nature.

Rebellion: If a woman is angry with parents, a lover, husband, or friends, and is not expressing her feelings openly, she may be likely to act out her feelings instead of communicating them, and get pregnant "to show them!" Getting pregnant is not a good way to resist someone else's authority. New life is a joy when we invite it from a loving and peaceful place within. Bringing a child into an angry and burdened environment can only add to our conflicts. It is better to express our anger directly. Assertiveness training can be of great help. If we learn to ask for what we need and fulfill our desires constructively, we do not need to rebel. Once we truly feel we are free, that is, once we create our own freedom, rebellion is no longer necessary. Entering into relationships freely with strength and dignity, sure of who we are and what we want, allows us to know if having a child is the best choice for us now, later, or never.

In a rut: Once in a while, we all get into a rut. Sometimes, when a woman's aspirations for professional work are obstructed or seem unattainable, the thought of pregnancy may become very appealing—if only to bring change. Actually, following through on this desire to have a child when we are feeling as if we are treading water and just need change, may not be what we need most for our own self-development. Having a child is an event that will demand the re-ordering of your life. Childrearing demands ongoing creativity, and once a woman takes on this responsibility, it is a long-term commitment.

Competing and Comparing: Each woman finds her fulfillment in different ways at different times. Childbearing is one kind of fulfillment, but certainly not the only one a woman can have. A woman may find herself to be the only childless woman in her circle of friends, or perhaps her best friend has just become pregnant. The question, "Do I want children?" may come up. When our friends become pregnant, they begin to experience a new relationship we cannot share. Sometimes priorities shift so much after a pregnancy there may be no time to share mutual interests for a while. Our friendships have to grow and change as we do, and adapting to changing situations enhances our relationships. This way our lives are enriched by the closeness that can come from sharing thoughts and feelings about such an important event as pregnancy, and our friend's life can be enriched by maintaining activities other than caring for children or preparing for childbirth. Sharing in the joy of a friend's pregnancy, possibly being present at the birth, and even making a commitment to share in the responsibility of caring for the child can be a practical and meaningful expression of friendship. Letting go of the tendency to judge ourselves by someone else's time cycle can leave room to share in the joys of all of our friends. The roots of self-love and self-acceptance are the foundation for the love and acceptance of others.

Testing the Man: It is far more common these days to have an ongoing sexual relationship without mention of commitment, much less marriage. A woman may be vaguely aware that she wants something more than a here and now relationship, but she is either not clear in her own mind about this, or feels uncomfortable about sharing her thoughts and feelings on the subject with her partner. Either she says nothing or what she does say still leaves the question open. An unplanned pregnancy can certainly force a man to clarify where he stands. A woman may harbor the fantasy that becoming pregnant will prove to her and to the man that they really care for each other. If a couple is not able to express their feelings openly, a pregnancy will not necessarily change that or bring them closer. In fact, it may complicate matters as confused feelings arise. Often a woman is unsure about whether she feels ready to have a child. By talking together and communicating openly, she can work out the conflict with her partner, rather than by herself. Even if a woman is ready for a commitment and a child, the man may not be. It is better for both to talk this out in advance rather than take a chance and see if it will all work out. The easiest way for a woman to know where a man stands is to simply ask. Taking the risk of asking may be difficult, but going through an unnecessary abortion or basing a pregnancy on a chancy relationship is much more traumatic.

Excitement: People take risks in different ways, some by driving race cars or skiing down Mt. Everest—others risk pregnancy. To some, sex may seem more exciting when the possibility of pregnancy exists, but it's a lot like playing with fire—you can get burned. Since three abortions or more may result in an increased risk of miscarriage in a later pregnancy, it is wiser to satisfy the need for thrills in another way, and leave reproductive risk-taking alone. Spontaneous surrender may be fun, and being caught without a contraceptive while sailing to Tahiti can happen—but there is no need to make a habit of it.

Maternal Instinct: Nobody—psychologists, scientists, sociologists—agrees as to whether a maternal instinct does or does not exist in women. Is there an inherent biological need to bear a child? Many women have never experienced a strong desire to bear a child, and feel completely fulfilled leading professional lives. Other women, though, have experienced strong bodily urges to bear a child. One woman said, "At one point in my life I experienced my body craving a child. I knew on a rational level that the time was not the best for me, but my body's message was so strong that I gave in to it.[31]

Experts who recognize this urge account for it in two different ways. Esther Harding notes in her book, *Psychic Energy*, that in contrast to the theme of a child's need to free her or himself from the bonds of the mother and father, little attention has been paid in the psychological literature to a woman's struggle to free herself from the bonds of her own maternal instinct. She says:

> The desire for children may be but the expression of an instinct whose sole purpose is the satisfaction of a biological need, and unless it is brought into a meaningful and conscious relation to the woman's total personality it will remain without psychological or emotional value. Such a woman is in danger of falling under the daemonic pow-

er of the maternal instinct that impels her to bear children, whom she will then regard as merely adjuncts to herself, possessions without individual or human rights.

In contrast, researcher Dr. Frederick Wyatte, says, "When a woman says with feeling that she craved her baby from within, she is putting into biological language what is psychological."[32]

Dr. William Goode attributes the desire for children to social pressure, "There are reflexes, like eye-blinking, and drives, like sex. There is no innate drive for children. Otherwise, the enormous cultural pressures that there are to reproduce wouldn't exist."[33]

Theories which support or deny the existence of a strong maternal urge in women are of no consequence when we are experiencing the power of this desire. What to do? First we must face and accept this yearning within ourselves—to try to forget about it or ignore it in the hopes it will go away is not going to help. Avoidance of any strong feeling may, in fact, allow this feeling more power over us on an unconscious level. One of the most common causes of an unplanned pregnancy is a woman's neglecting to resolve attitudes of ambivalence towards childbearing.

For those women who *do* want to have children at some point in their lives, it is important for them and their future children to prepare for this event by making room for a new relationship in their lives.

It's okay (and healthy) to recognize the fact that, although you may want a child sometime in the future, you do not right now. What muddles our thinking and actions is indecision as to whether or not now is a good time. There are some good ways we can examine our desire to have a child now. Some of these are visiting mothers, taking care of someone else's children, and going on a guided fantasy trip to explore the extent to which your life would change if you did have a child now. These are considered in the next section.

WAYS TO DEVELOP HEALTHIER ATTITUDES

Attitudes that diminish our strength, energy, and our joy in living need not continue indefinitely. There are things we can do to re-frame negative ways of thinking and behaving and make room for more positive and creative attitudes. Ambivalence and indecision can be uncomfortable, as well as contributing factors to becoming pregnant. The following are a few suggestions I have found to be particularly helpful to women in sorting out their feelings and thoughts toward motherhood.

Visiting Mothers: If you do not have any friends who have children, you can easily meet mothers through your local woman's center. It would be helpful to talk to women who have a lifestyle similar to yours so you can see how they handle the maternal role. Ask these women how they enjoy their children and their role as mothers, how children have changed their lives, how their priorities were readjusted, what unexpected changes they needed to make, and what difficulties, if any, they experience with their children. Usually mothers are only too happy to share their experiences with other women who might be considering having children. If some questions seem to make a woman uncomfortable, just listen to what she is willing to share. Often, in our fantasy life, we imagine motherhood very different from what it is. Remember, though, that no two women experience mothering in exactly the same way. Talking with mothers can bring our attention to areas of experience we may have never considered previously.

Caring for a Child: One of the best ways to get in touch with your feelings toward motherhood is to get some "real world" experience. Offering to care for someone else's child can familiarize you with a child's physical and emotional needs and help you consider how (and if) you can fulfill these needs. You can ask yourself: Do I feel comfortable with the non-verbal communication so necessary and natural between myself and this child? Do I recognize how my feelings and moods affect this child? Do I enjoy the rewards a small child gives—the openness to experience, the sense of wonder and exploration, trust, and spontaneity? Do I feel okay about the child's demands for my attention?

If you feel burdened by or resentful toward small children, chances are you do not have the energy right now to give a young child what she or he needs. It is possible a particular child is more demanding than other children. Many parents feel it is easier to give to and be tolerant of their own children than their friends' children. You must evaluate your experiences and your reactions very carefully.

If you feel the need, it may be possible to do something to develop your capacity to nurture and enjoy a small child. A good way to prepare for mothering is to volunteer time at a good child care center. Skilled pre-school teachers have a wealth of knowledge any mother or father can benefit from. Parenting is one of the most important roles any adult can assume in society, and it is an area to which our educational system devotes very little time and money. We can initiate change for ourselves and for others, by insisting on parent training as part of ongoing educational curricula.

Guided Fantasy: Fantasies make use of our imagination. It allows us to explore future consequences of remaining or becoming pregnant. This technique is most fruitful if you select a time you can relax and take as long as you need to become aware of your feelings. Ask a friend to read the following instructions to you. This person should be someone stable whom you trust, so that if you become aware of some deep, or uncomfortable emotions you can feel free to express them. Agree beforehand on a method you will use to signal your friend when you are ready for the next instruction. Some images may arise and pass quickly; others may take a longer time to "feel through." Lie down in a warm and comfortable room. Close your eyes and just relax for five minutes. Deep breathing or possibly remembering a quiet time or place you enjoyed may help you relax. Then your friend begins to say the following:

• "You are pregnant. Let the warm and lovely feelings come through as well as the scarey and unexpected feelings."

• "You are now telling the important people in your life that you are pregnant. How do you feel telling them? How do they respond to the news?"

• "You are beginning to show now. How does this affect your job, or your schooling?"

• "It is now the last month. You are preparing for the new baby. Will you be able to continue your normal routine? Must you quit your job or schooling? How will you support yourself?"

• "The baby is being born. Allow yourself to feel whatever comes up."

• "It is time to continue your life now as a mother. How will you work out a balance between caring for your child and for your own needs. Who is there to help you care for the child?"

• "How much involvement does the father of the child offer? What is the quality of your relationship with him?"

• "How does your social life change? If you want to go out who will care for the baby?"

• "Slowly allow yourself to come back to the here and now and stay with the emotion you feel most strongly right now."

• "Is it a strong affirmation, or negation of wanting to be pregnant, of wanting the child? What else? Do you have mixed feelings?"

Consciousness-Raising Groups are groups of people coming together on a regular basis to share experiences and support each other through change. If it is a woman's group, each woman is expected to contribute to the group and make a commitment to attend for a certain period of time. Consciousness raising is not therapy in the traditional sense of the word. Usually one woman does not become the group leader. The responsibility for the group process is shared by each member of the group, sometimes alternately, sometimes together. In such a supportive environment a woman can learn to gradually trust her own feelings and experiences by expressing and clarifying them. Also, each woman learns from the variety of feelings and experiences that the others bring to the group. Through group trust and sharing, a woman can see new possibilities as to how she can make her life and relationships more meaningful.

Counseling: Traditionally, the majority of counselors were men and the majority of their clients were women. Now, however, there are many more women entering the psychological and counseling professions. One new trend in the helping professions is that of feminist therapy. The basis of this therapy is the affirmation of a woman's wholeness, her feeling that she is unique as a feminine being. During this process, constricting social roles and views are confronted and left behind, making room for greater self-fulfillment and a more real contribution to society. The techniques used may include Gestalt therapy, sensory awareness, dream exploration, and body awareness. We must feel our own power emerging from within our feminine bodies. Feeling at home in our bodies allows us to accept our womanliness and express our feminine energy in many ways. "Feminism" also encourages men and women to grow beyond social roles and attitudes which restrict their full development. Feminist therapy encourages a woman to develop strength and to take responsibility for her life while enjoying being a woman. An excellent book to read on the subject is *Feminism as Therapy* by Anica Vesel Mander and Anne Kent Rush.

Women's Studies is a rapidly growing new field in colleges and universities. The purpose of women's programs is to recognize and study the contributions women have made to culture throughout time, to develop an understanding of the effect of social roles on the lives of individual women, and to gain an appreciation of the psychology of women. Such programs are enriching and strengthening for women (and men) of any age. Educational materials have, in past years, been predominantly male-oriented. Women's studies provided us with the knowledge and pride that women have developed their talent, have individuated themselves, and have contributed to society, often in the face of tremendous obstacles. Women through the ages have struggled against far greater obstacles than we encounter today. Understanding and appreciating the rich contributions of women to the world gives us greater appreciation and respect for women's talents and their influence and role in shaping culture and ideas.

Assertiveness Training: Throughout this book I have spoken of taking responsibility for our lives. Growing up female in this culture has traditionally taught us to be passive and to make the best of our lot. When we set out to change a situation in our lives, we use our power to institute change in our environment. Often we do not know how to use our power in a positive and creative way. Assertiveness training through role playing and a series of exercises, can help a woman learn how and become more comfortable with, asserting herself. Byrna Taubman in *How To Become An Assertive Woman* says:

> Learning assertiveness is learning to ask yourself, "What do I want? What do I need? What do I need to ask for? How can I ask for that without making a demand? How can I make it clear that this is important to me?"

Women's Centers vary in the time and energy they invest in different activities. Some centers run bookstores, childcare facilities, drop-in rap groups, on-going consciousness raising groups, and classes in self-help. Centers are organized to serve the needs of women in a spirit of compassion and sharing. A wealth of information is usually available from the women themselves and/or from their library and programs on birth control, abortion, and other subjects relating directly to women. Usually a complete list of community resources is also available. All questions and feelings shared are respected, and so is confidentiality.

Self-help Groups can be created wherever there are women who want to learn more about their own bodies and develop the knowledge and power to take good care of their own health needs. Often a few women in the group are already well-versed in the areas of physiology, reproduction, and sexuality, but each woman can make a contribution by sharing her experiences. Some of the skills taught include: how to use a speculum to examine one's cervix, detecting very early signs of pregnancy or discovering cervical cancer before it has time to spread. Breast exam and pelvic exam are also learned. Knowing our own bodies and keeping ourselves healthy is a practical application of self-determination. The women in each self-help group decide together which topic(s) interest them most and study these in greater depth. Birth control and abortion are usually discussed quite extensively.

Women's Health Collectives are a natural outgrowth of the advanced self-help groups. After developing a degree of expertise in the field of woman's health, it was natural for women to want to make this knowledge available to as many other women as possible. Women paramedics have been trained to provide services such as administering pap smears, detecting venereal disease, determining pregnancy, detecting special uterine characteristics, birth control counseling, midwifery, and pre- and postnatal care. The women who collectively run these clinics hire doctors who meet their standards for professional competence and sensitivity to women's needs. Often abortions are performed as part of their services and, if not, abortion referrals are available. See Appendix III for information on how to start your own local women's health collective.

Women and Imagery: Images accompanied by strong feelings sometimes emerge from the deep layers of one's psyche. When these images are not simply reflections of everyday objects or events, but point beyond themselves to an internal event, they are called symbols. The "mother" symbol has appeared in art and literature throughout time and cultures to represent certain feminine qualities, such as creativity and nurturance. It may happen that a woman becomes deeply moved by the "mother" symbol and this may have nothing to do with physical maternity but rather psychological maternity. The psyche is a source of new life—new ideas, new hopes, new possibilities—all of which can be given form by investing the time, energy, and knowledge necessary.

The maternal image may arise in dreams, or as a product of a creative imagination exercise, or spontaneously emerge through an everyday activity. It is not always an easy process to sort out the desire for physical motherhood from the desire to give birth to one's own latent potentials. Study and guidance are necessary to become skilled in utilizing any imagery which may arise. Developing the capacity for abstract thinking allows us to look through the obvious into the more subtle layers of existence. A more in-depth discussion of dream analysis and other symbolic processes is beyond the scope of this book, but there are many good books on dreams and symbols which can be very helpful. Among these are June Singer's *Boundaries of the Soul* and Mary Esther Harding's *Women's Mytheries*. Investigating our personal imagery can broaden our awareness of life's possibilities and give us new directions for our journey towards wholeness.

My own work in this field of symbolic processes has taught me that the "mother" symbol can point towards the need for nurturance. A woman's own need to be nurtured continues through life. Touching is a basic human need, as is love, acceptance, and play. If the "mother" image arises within us, it may mean that we are not mothering the child within us enough. Massage, saunas, or a day at the beach, are a few ways a woman can nurture herself. The "mother" image may also mean a woman is growing towards the capacity to nurture others on a professional level. All of the helping professions require a balance between knowledge, skill and an expertise on one hand and compassion, caring, and sensitivity on the other. One woman, after an abortion, discovered that her feminine qualities could have professional value in helping others. She says:

> By becoming a preschool teacher, I integrated my need for developing my own potentials with my need for time alone to heal the wounds of my own upbringing. If I had become a mother five years ago, I believe, I would have still had the space to develop my intuitive-feeling capacities, but I could not have had the same experience of these capacities being okay parts of me as a woman, not just as a mother. I also have had the opportunity to integrate my felt-experiences with my rational, focused consciousness.[34]

It is helpful to be aware that the "mother" image can point towards a psychological maternity as well as a physical maternity.

Meditation is an excellent adjunct to any of the previously mentioned resources. There are many forms of this ancient tool for developing consciousness. From my own experience, I have found the Transcendental Meditation technique which was brought to the West in 1958 by Maharishi Mahesh Yogi, to be the most beneficial and universally applicable. TM is unlike other forms of meditation in that it does not involve concentration nor contemplation. The natural tendency of the mind itself is utilized in a very effortless way. Practiced 15–20 minutes twice daily, TM causes a profoundly unique state of neurophysiological functioning. The body is more deeply resting than during deep sleep and yet the mind becomes very alert. This "restful alertness" is not only very enjoyable in itself but it also enlivens the nervous system and reorders the brain waves to a more coherent pattern. As a result of regular meditation, a person feels more physical energy, emotional stability, and mental clarity as well as continuing to grow in the qualities which humankind has throughout the centuries held most dear—these qualities developed to their fullness describes the state of enlightenment. This type of meditation has been researched more thoroughly (300 studies in 29 countries) for its positive benefits than any other mental techniques ancient or modern. Fatigue, stress and strain are blocks to the realization of our full potential. TM removes these barriers and therefore helps a person meet the demands of daily life more gracefully as well as strengthens the nervous system and psyche to be able to deal with challenging circumstances (such as those that an unplanned pregnancy presents) with greater ease and efficiency.

Not all forms of meditation are equally beneficial or even safe. One helpful clue for choosing a form of meditation is investigating the history of the technique to be sure it is time-tested and reliable. The TM technique originates from the very ancient Vedic tradition which is thousands of years old.

Most women I know who have been practicing the TM technique for at least six months (in many cases less than that) notice a dramatic increase in self-affirmation, ease in developing their own talents, and an increasing ability to balance independence with caring for others. The growth that occurs through the practice of the TM technique is natural, spontaneous, and wholistic. This meditation is the most basic form of self-nurturance and the most enjoyable tool for developing self-actualization that I know. See references in Suggested Reading list.

CHAPTER SIX

Contraception
and Prevention

The use of contraception obviously demands that women feel at ease with themselves, their bodies, and their lovers, and also be able to accept some of the less romantic aspects of bodily functions.

Kristen Luker

EACH WOMAN, FROM ADOLESCENCE ONWARDS is faced with many opportunities to express her sexuality with a male partner. Whether a woman is fifteen and deciding if she is ready for her first experience of intercourse or forty and happily married, there are many factors which can make the prevention of an unwanted pregnancy a difficult task. For years risk-taking women who did not use any form of birth control were considered proper candidates for psychological counseling (masochistic, unconsciously wanting a child, etc.). In *Taking Chances*, Kristen Luker poses a sociological explanation for women's risk-taking. She points out that skiing and smoking cigarettes are socially accepted forms of risk-taking. Since over 50 percent of women take contraceptive chances at some time in their lives, it can hardly be considered deviant. She suggests that a woman's non-use of birth control is the result of a reasoning process in which a woman weighs the apparent costs of using birth control against the cost of an unwanted pregnancy. In Chapter Eight, I will discuss the attitudes which can contribute to an unwanted pregnancy. In this chapter I wish to deal with the costs of birth control. Prevention of unwanted pregnancies is not as simple as it may appear.

The question, "Why doesn't a woman just use birth control?" is answerable only by exploring our cultural-social attitudes towards sexuality, and by understanding the difficulties women still experience when seeking out birth control information and supplies. Each of us is responsible for our own sexual and contraceptive decisions. There are, however, many complexities which lie between ourselves as responsible women, and the fulfillment of our responsibility to prevent unwanted pregnancies.

Why is all this important in a book on abortion? Very simple—our view of our sexuality has an important influence on our use of contraceptives and *this* has a lot to do with the subject of abortion. When I say "our" use of contraceptives I am not referring only to women. This includes men and women —"society." Contraceptive information is still not readily available. Contraceptives are not always easy to get and the available forms of contraceptives all have their disadvantages.

Knowledge of the various methods of contraceptives, the pros and cons for each and how to use them is essential information for every young person to have before blossoming into fertility. But even contraceptive expertise is not enough. The technological know-how for preventing unwanted pregnancies is largely ineffectual if one has not accepted one's sexuality or feels guilty about sexual feelings. Taking responsibility for birth control can follow naturally upon the healthy acceptance of one's sexuality.

Our society flaunts sex to our young people even through such supposedly non-sexual advertisements as cigarette ads! Note the attitude of acceptance that permits dress and seductive presentation of most ads on tv, yet simultaneously forbids sex and birth control education in the schools. No wonder women report their early sexual experiences in these words, "It just happened." We consider an act more "sinful" or "punishable" if it is committed with full knowledge and forethought. Preventing unwanted pregnancies *demands* such knowledge and thought.

Minors no longer need the consent of their parents to have an abortion. Yet the adult community is essentially denying minors the right to the information necessary to prevent abortion.

Until January of 1976, it was still illegal in the state of California to give birth control information to minors. There is now a wealth of knowledge on human sexuality. Is it not the school's responsibility to provide birth control information along with sex education and possibly provide classes for parents also, to help them learn how to talk to their children about sex?

In every other field of human knowledge we would think it absurd to make the new generation learn for themselves from scratch. But in the field of sexuality we pretend we don't have any organized body of knowledge that can be passed down and allow young people to bypass some of our mistakes.

A middle-aged mother, upon hearing her fifteen-year-old daughter had recently faced an unwanted pregnancy and an abortion alone, broke into tears, "How I wish I could have been of help. Twenty years ago I went through an illegal abortion myself. I know what she must have gone through." Parents often do not share their own feelings and knowledge about sexuality, birth control, and abortion with their children because of their own unresolved conflicts. One young man upon reaching his eighteenth birthday was taken into his parents' bedroom by his father. The father threw him a pack of condoms and said, "If you're going to get laid, use one of these. And remember, if you ever get a girl pregnant, don't come home." It is small wonder the young man suffered an acute case of anxiety after each experience of sexual intercourse for many years afterwards. Avoiding the issue of sexuality can only encourage a young person to seek answers elsewhere. Elsewhere, whether it be a friend or a book, may or may not be a reliable source. Any teenager realizes that adults avoid what is uncomfortable for them.

Feelings about sexuality begin to be communicated to a child from infancy. Unfortunately, a parent must either accept her or his own sexuality in a healthy way, or pass the conflict along to her or his children. A parent is either part of the solution by sharing healthy sexual attitudes and knowledge appropriate to a child's level of development, or is part of the problem by avoiding the issue or displaying a negative attitude about sexuality. Even if a parent has unresolved feelings about sexuality (which is not uncommon) it is more helpful to admit these conflicts to a daughter or son and provide good reading material. One of the best books available for parents and teachers is *High School Sexuality—A Teaching Guide*, prepared by the Women's Educational Project.

Young people are not the only ones who have erroneous birth control information. Many women and men still operate under the assumption that the rhythm method is an effective means of birth control. I have heard the comment often, "I just don't understand it. The only time I made love with my husband last month was during my period. How could I be pregnant?" Masters and Johnson have found that a few women ovulate at any time in their cycle as a physiological response to the excitement of intercourse. We need complete and current birth control information to be available to everyone. One way is through the mass media: television, radio, newspapers, if it is communicated by qualified people. One of the reasons this has not yet happened is the fear that the more people know about birth control, the more sexual promiscuity there will be. Parents and teachers fear the same. However, if parents and schools would communicate information about sex and birth control to children and adolescents, and through mass media to adults, at least people could make informed choices rather than act impulsively without fully understanding the consequences of their behavior.

We are all caught up in a sexual transition. Our American forefathers preached that sex was evil, sinful and tolerable (at best) for procreation. Our American tribal drum—the television—beats out the rhythm of sex to sell everything from cars to toothpaste. Most of us grew up with some religious influence in our homes which coincided with the recurring glow of the tv set. It is the rare individual who has escaped the resulting conflicts of opposing ideas, feelings, and actions in regards to sexuality. Is sex good? Is sex bad? Is sex natural? Is sex instinctual? Is sex spiritual? Do I enjoy sex? Am I afraid of sex? Do I put up with sex? Do I avoid sex? These are some of the unresolved questions people have grown up with.

How we use and express our sexuality is a matter of individual responsibility and choice. Our culture gives very little sanction or support for expression of human sexuality. Our Judaeo-Christian roots have emphasized sexuality as having a distinct purpose, "to be fruitful and multiply." Until recently any woman making a conscious choice to express her sexuality outside of the context of childbearing within marriage, experienced her own inner resistance or social pressure. Catholic marriage manuals regarded an intentionally childless marriage as sinful; the Talmud compares the lack of children to death; generally speaking a childless couple was considered selfish if they chose to remain childless or were pitied if they were infertile.

Now that society's attitudes have changed, we are beginning to acknowledge our sexuality as an end in itself—pleasure—and as a means for expressing love and intimacy. Sexuality exists as a human experience prior to either a stable heterosexual relationship or marriage. At last we are able to recognize that sexual feelings exist from infancy through the golden years. Sexual activity is not limited to sexual intercourse. Erogenous zones can be located on our ears, our feet, our fingers and nose. Masturbation is a normal result of self-exploration. If we feel guilty about our sexual feelings, this will affect any sexual relationship we become involved in (including marriage). Feeling guilty about our sexuality contributes significantly to unwanted pregnancies, which has been one of the socially accepted forms of self-punishment for engaging in "illicit" relationships (only for women of course!).

Accepting our sexuality is the beginning of a creation of our sexual identity. Sexual identity includes an acceptance of one's sexual energy as well as the choice to express this energy within the context of one's life. If a woman is able to find sexual pleasure and fulfillment for herself, then she is able to enter a sexual relationship with a man with the possibility of feeling independent and fulfilled. A full discussion of female sexuality is beyong the scope of this book. Two sources which may be helpful are Lonnie Barbach's *For Yourself*, and Barbara Seaman's *Free and Female*.

Answering the following questions can help you gain insight into some aspects of your sexual identity as it exists right now.
• When was the first time you experienced a sexual feeling?
• How did you feel about it? Did you allow yourself to feel the pleasure? Did you cut off the good feelings?
• Have you ever felt guilty about spontaneous sexual feelings?
• When was the first time you masturbated? Did you feel okay about it?
• Do you masturbate now? Do you feel okay about it?
• Do you feel comfortable talking about sexuality with your family, friends, sexual partner?
• Are you able to satisfy your sexual needs for yourself and/or within your sexual relationship(s)?

Many of us only let ourselves feel physical pleasure in the context of love-making. This habit localizes the sensual experience in the genital area. The more a person allows the life energy to flow freely throughout one's whole body the more generalized the experience of pleasure becomes. Running, swimming, laughing, listening to music, smelling a rose, and eating, can be very pleasurable experiences. Living is a multi-sensual phenomenon. Becoming alive to all of our senses is becoming awake to life. If we expand our capacity for pleasure—for enjoying all of life—then our sexual experiences become one of the many possible ways we can enjoy our bodies.

One special way of giving and receiving pleasure is through touching. Touching not only feels good, it is a necessity of life. Babies who are deprived of cuddling and caressing can die. Some families may freely hug and hold young children but not older children. Touching is a direct expression of loving and caring. Women tend to feel freer to show each other physical affection within a friendship than do men. Touching can be a spontaneous greeting, a source of comfort, or an art.

The art of touching is massage. There are many forms of massage. Some are simple to learn, like "Esalen massage," which uses simple strokes along the natural alignment of the muscles. Others require more skill such as polarity massage. Often, our need for simple touching or a good massage is far greater than our sexual needs. If our bodies become tense, we not only cut off pleasure but also the very life energy flowing through us. Massage is one way of showing our love and one of the most fulfilling ways to enjoy our bodies.

Learning how to give ourselves pleasure in a distinctly sexual way can only increase our ability to gain satisfaction in a sexual relationship with another. Once we learn to give pleasure to ourselves we can more easily learn to ask for what feels good to us from a sexual partner. When we establish our sexual identity independent from a relationship, we are more likely to establish relationships with others on the grounds of appreciation and caring rather than from the position of need for sexual satisfaction.

If we accept our own sexuality and feel okay about enjoying sexual pleasure, we have then grown beyond the sexual conflict that exists in America today. Each woman who feels comfortable with her sexuality has usually achieved this harmony through a conscious decision to integrate her sexuality into the wholeness of her life. Most often a woman has sought support from others who are also making this transition, and may have used a variety of techniques including consciousness-raising, body work, sex therapy, feminist counseling. These methods are discussed in Chapter

Five. If we choose to express our sexuality with a male partner as most women do, then we must address ourselves to the question of birth control.

The best place to go for birth control is a woman's health center or a Planned Parenthood clinic. A woman's health center is a woman-controlled center offering health care services which relate specifically to the reproductive system—although other services may also be available. Both Planned Parenthood and a woman's health center usually offer classes in birth control methods that help each woman decide which method is best for her. Each method of birth control has some negative side effects and just how negative those side effects are for you cannot always be determined until you try it. It helps to understand the pros and cons of all birth control methods so you can change to another method, should one not prove right for you and your partner. If you go to a gynecologist for birth control do not depend on him or her for complete information on your chosen method or on your options. Many women have become pregnant or have hurt their bodies relying on the limited information certain doctors give. One woman said:

> The doctor told me the IUD was safe and sure and I should check the string once in a while. Only after I became pregnant did I learn that a backup method should be used in the first three months after IUD insertion and that checking the string by feeling into the vagina could not tell me if it had moved too far back or too far forward in the uterus. Only seeing how long the string is upon insertion and checking once a week with speculum and mirror is a sure way to know that the IUD is still in place.[35]

Even though the private gynecologist is one of the major sources for birth control supplies, it would help if you inform yourself fully *before* entering the doctor's office. Even if your doctor is very well known and well respected this does not prevent him/her from having a certain bias towards a particular birth control method. Some doctors are notorious for pressuring women into a certain birth control choice or for withholding information on the side effects of their favorite method. Being informed before you enter the office can also help you evaluate the ethics and knowledge of the doctor you are seeing.

Sometimes we must wait for appointments at our doctor's office or local clinic. There is therefore a delay that exists between the time a woman decides she wants to use a birth control method and the time she actually gains access to that method. In some places a woman must be very persistent to get birth control at all, especially if she is a minor, or if the chosen method is sterilization.

Health services need to be expanded to serve the needs of the people in every area. Until that happens, a woman may need to change doctors or drive to a clinic some distance from her home. If you are successful in obtaining birth control but still have some doubts concerning its proper use, don't hesitate to ask your doctor, nurse, or clinic counselor. You owe it to yourself to understand clearly all the instructions relating to your method. No birth control method works if it is used improperly. Your partner, if you are only involved with one person, may wish to go with you to find out the different methods and to understand correct use, as part of his responsibility.

Health professionals can help prevent abortion by offering better and more complete and easily accessible birth control classes which meet frequently. Publicity is important. The people in a community need to know that services are available before they can benefit from them. Outreach programs are usually as successful as educational programs in the schools. Operating a facility on a drop-in basis is very important. Birth control can only be available to everyone through increased awareness of all the options, and acceptance by individuals that their sexuality, as well as their desire to use birth control, is healthy.

There is still a lot of work to be done before birth control will be available to every woman in this country. Transforming our frustrations into creating new options for ourselves and other women seems to be the most effective answer. One of the best ways to increase the availability of birth control is to establish a local self-help group which can grow into a woman's health collective. See the Appendix III for details.

Ideally, a contraceptive choice should be made prior to a woman's (or a man's) first experience of sexual intercourse. However, the initial choice of a method may change at a later time. All methods have their rates of failure and their disadvantages. The most effective methods of birth control are female oriented (the pill and the IUD) and are also the most threatening to a woman's health. The least threatening to one's health are methods which are, unfortunately, less effective in preventing pregnancy. Natural birth control is couple-oriented and is becoming increasingly popular. There is a high success rate for some of the methods, and they demand much more time, planning, and responsibility on the part of the users. Each contraceptive choice presents its conflicts. If one or more methods have not worked well for a woman or if a method has caused serious side effects, this narrows her contraceptive options and her desire to use birth control. Unresolved conflict about any contraceptive choice may result in inconsistent use of that method, and pregnancy.

Risking an unwanted pregnancy can only cause a woman to feel tension during sexual intercourse. This can soon lead to a feeling of alienation from one's body because "it won't do what I want it to do,"—that is, my body will not remain unpregnant naturally. Ultimately this can destroy pleasure in sexual intercourse and lead to feelings of anger and resentment.

For most women one or more methods of birth control do work satisfactorily and do reduce the risk of an unwanted pregnancy considerably. Using no birth control is hardly a risk—it will very likely lead to pregnancy; 80-90 percent of women who use no birth control become pregnant. The time varies from woman to woman. Some women become pregnant the first time they have sex, other women become pregnant only after several years of sexual activity. There is no way a woman can determine beforehand whether she will become pregnant sooner or later.

Sexual intercourse is not even always necessary to become pregnant. If any of the man's semen reaches the woman's vaginal lips through mutual touching or caressing, it is possible for sperm to move through the vagina through the woman's mucus and finally arrive in the tubes where fertilization can take place.

A woman may think that the longer she takes chances successfully the more likely it is this good luck will continue. This is *not* true and is a naive attitude. In fact, the likelihood of becoming pregnant increases with the number of chances a woman takes.

Many women have been told by their gynecologists that they may have trouble conceiving due to the shape or position of the womb or any number of other reasons. This information is no insurance against pregnancy. In fact, the greater majority of women who were discouraged about their possible infertility and did not use birth control soon found out that they were indeed fertile. If a woman desires to confirm her fertility, it is self-destructive to go through an unwanted pregnancy or abortion to find out. Becoming pregnant and then aborting does not prove that one's body could carry a child to term, nor does having one abortion seriously threaten the chances of carrying a child to term in the future. If you are sure you do not want to bear a child now, you can possibly observe your fertility through your vaginal mucus. Each time a woman ovulates the vagina discharges clear, slippery, shiny mucus which has the consistency of egg white. By observing our daily mucus, we become more in harmony with our body's cycle and can in fact learn to prevent pregnancy through one of the natural methods mentioned later.

A woman and a man can become more fertile through changes in diet and lifestyle which decrease tension and increase general health. Vitamin E, especially, can increase fertility. Some women have become pregnant soon after eliminating such habits as smoking or drinking too much alcohol. (Please do not think that poor diet and bad health habits are any guarantee of infertility!) We owe it to ourselves and all the children we may plan to have to be as healthy as possible.

Preventing unwanted pregnancies is the mutual responsibility of a sexually active couple. Most often the woman feels the responsibility to use birth control more than the man. A man can help prevent unwanted pregnancies by taking the time to learn about the different methods of birth control and then asking a woman which method she is using. If a woman is using an unreliable means of birth control the man can discuss this with her, help her examine her motives; he can use a condom and suggest that the woman use foam simultaneously, which gives close to 100 percent protection. He can also help her make a different contraceptive choice, if she so desires. If a man takes precautions to avoid an unwanted pregnancy, this can only enhance the feelings of trust and caring in the relationship. Ideally, a couple should discuss birth control before sexual intercourse. Sharing feelings about contraception and sharing the costs and responsibilities of whichever method seems best is a very practical expression of intimacy which more couples are now able to participate in. If a man does not ask you if you are using birth control, or is not willing to discuss the subject, it might be worth your while to question his integrity.

The contraceptive riddle is a hard one to solve. No single answer seems to work for every woman. The following descriptions of birth control methods is by no means exhaustive, nor are they meant to be. No woman reading this book should base a contraceptive choice solely on the limited information available here. Throughout this section I have attempted to include a few basic facts about each method and information I have learned through my research. The most comprehensive descriptions of birth control methods can be found in the book *Our Bodies, Ourselves* written by the Boston Women's Health Collective. Other books which deal with a particular method are mentioned in the appropriate sections and in Suggested Reading.

NON-METHODS

The following methods for preventing pregnancy do not work and should not be attempted by anyone who is seriously trying to avoid conception.
• If you are already breastfeeding an infant, this is no guarantee against pregnancy. Ovulation occurs before the first period following pregnancy so there will be no warning unless you are practicing the Ovulation Method mentioned later.
• Pre-menopausal women must still be cautious.
• Douching can only increase the likelihood of pregnancy by shooting sperm up the vaginal canal and through the oss.
• Withdrawal is not only difficult to accomplish but if any seminal fluid leaks out before ejaculation (which almost always happens) then a pregnancy can result.
• Avoiding orgasm only prevents pleasure, not pregnancy.
• Calendar rhythm—few people can rely on the rhythm methods. The rest have unplanned pregnancies.
• Intercourse during a menstrual period is unsafe.

EASY-TO-GET METHODS

The following can be purchased at almost any pharmacy by anyone of any age without a prescription.
Condoms are made of latex rubber or animal skin, they fit snuggly over the erect penis and catch the seminal fluid so that it does not enter the vagina. For condoms to be effective they must be

used from the beginning of sexual intercourse before any genital contact has been made. They must be put on carefully to avoid tears and holes and must have one-half inch extra at the tip to prevent bursting when the seminal fluid is released. They must be removed carefully so that the contents do not spill into the vagina. While the penis is withdrawn the condom must be held in place. Petroleum jelly should never be used with condoms as it may cause the rubber to deteriorate. Only contraceptive jellies or contraceptive foams should be used with condoms. Since the penis is softer after intercourse, the condom can slip off and be left behind. Condoms are somewhat of a nuisance, sometimes considered unaesthetic, and by themselves are between 80-97 percent effective. Some men claim condoms cut down on sensation, "It's like taking a shower with a raincoat on." Others strongly deny this. Men are actually getting back to using condoms and enjoying them:

> I really love using condoms! Now I feel I'm really participating in birth control and saving my lady from using a method which might be hard on her body.[36]

Condoms used with contraceptive foam give close to 100 percent protection and involve both a man and woman in birth control. Many couples are learning to be very creative in incorporating this dual method in their foreplay.

Foam—Aerosol Vaginal Spermicide: Foam, by itself, is only 70 percent effective. It is easy to use: shake, fill applicator, and insert into vagina. Two applications should be used and directions should be read carefully. Some brands may be more irritating than others. It must be used within 15 minutes prior to sexual intercourse and another applicator-full must be inserted before each subsequent act of intercourse.

Jellies and Creams: Without a diaphragm, jellies and creams should never be used—they are highly ineffective. A diaphragm is obtainable only by prescription from a doctor.

PRESCRIPTION METHODS

The following methods must be obtained through a doctor's prescription or insertion (in the case of the IUD).

A *diaphragm* with jelly or cream is one of the oldest methods of female-oriented birth control. Margaret Sanger brought thousands of diaphragms into this country when she first began her contraceptive campaign. The diaphragm was invented in 1882 and many women used it throughout their fertile years without failure. This domed rubber device must be fitted by a doctor or health professional. Proper fit is absolutely essential for success. Two women who wear the same dress size will not necessarily use the same diaphragm size since the diaphragm is fit to the size of the cervix. Do not borrow a friend's diaphragm, it may not work for you. If a woman is still a virgin she may need a different size after a few experiences, since stretching will occur. After childbirth a woman may also need a new size. Gaining or losing ten pounds is ample reason to have your diaphragm size rechecked.

A diaphragm must always be used with a contraceptive cream or jelly, which is spread around the rim and in the center before inserting the diaphragm into the vagina. A tablespoon of jelly or cream is enough to use in the diaphragm. Spread it in the center and around the rim. The diaphragm must be left in for at least six to eight hours after intercourse. An additional applicator of cream or jelly must *again* be inserted before repeating intercourse. Stronger creams and jellies enhance effectiveness but may also be more irritating. Avoid all brands with mercury in them. Look for "mercuric . . . . " a multisyllabic ingredient printed on the label. Mercury can be absorbed into the body slowly, and over time become toxic.

Some women's anatomy does not allow a diaphragm to fit tightly. A poorly fitting diaphragm does not prevent pregnancy. To check the diaphragm fit, there are several things to look for. Be sure the rim of the diaphragm fits snuggly behind the pelvic bone and doesn't slip when pushing your finger between the rim and your bone. If your finger can dislodge the diaphragm so can a penis. The rim must also fit snugly against the vaginal walls on both sides and at the bottom. The cervix must be covered. If the diaphragm does not fit snugly, it may be too small. If there is too much rubber slack in the center of the diaphragm or you can feel the diaphragm when it is in place, then it may be too big. Some women have been fitted incorrectly by their physicians. One way to know you have the proper fit is to join a self-help group and learn how to check it yourself.

Despite the slight messiness and hassle that the diaphragm presents, and the chance that it can be dislodged during intercourse (especially a hazard when using fancy postures), the diaphragm is becoming ever more popular with women. Every year the diaphragm should be replaced. Old rubber cracks. Hold your diaphragm up to the light from time to time to be sure there are no holes or cracks. To care for your diaphragm, always wash it in luke-warm soap and water, and dry and powder with cornstarch. Keep it away from heat.

The details of using the diaphragm, including insertion and removal should be demonstrated and a woman should practice and feel confident before attempting to use her diaphragm for birth control. One of the most frequent causes of diaphragm failure is the incorrect insertion of the diaphragm into the vagina. If the diaphragm is inserted incorrectly, in front of the cervix, this can push the cervix down below the bottom rim of the diaphragm, which in fact increases the likelihood of pregnancy. Always angle downward when inserting the diaphragm.

There are three kinds of metal spring rims. The flat spring rim is much more difficult to insert correctly and therefore should be avoided. The coil and arcing metal spring rims are much easier to insert. Once a woman learns how to insert her diaphragm correctly it becomes very easy to continue to insert it correctly. Men, too, can learn how to insert the diaphragm correctly. However, each time a woman inserts her diaphragm, she should check to be sure the cervix is covered. Many women use a little extra contraceptive cream or jelly (about one tablespoon) just to be sure. The effectiveness rate of the diaphragm is between 85–97 percent.

IUD: The intrauterine device is inserted through the cervix into the uterus. Exactly how it works is still uncertain. The theories as to how it works are: by setting up a low-grade infection, implantation of the ovum is prevented; by introducing a foreign body in the uterus, the implanted zygote is soon expelled. Lippies Loop and the Saf-T-Coil are the safest IUDs. All IUDs can cause cramping, heavy bleeding, infection, can perforate the uterine wall, or can become dislodged—resulting in pregnancy. The string attached to the IUD should be checked every week using a speculum and mirror to be sure it is the same length. If the IUD moves too far back or forward in the uterus it may cease to be effective. Some women expel their IUDs spontaneously. This most frequently occurs during menstruation. Most women experience no ill effects and no pregnancies, but some do fail, cause problems, and/or cannot be tolerated by the woman. Women who have already borne a child have a better chance of maintaining an IUD. Some clinics will not even insert IUDs for women who have not yet had a child. Its effectiveness ranges from 93-99 percent. Long term effects are still unknown. Once the IUD is inserted (during or immediately after the menstrual period) its advantage is that nothing further needs to be done other than checking the string regularly, thus enhancing spontaneity. When taking antibiotics, it is advisable to use an additional method of birth control since the IUD's contraceptive effect may be diminished by the antibiotics, which are presumed to wipe out the low grade infection in the uterus the IUD causes.

The pill should be more thoroughly researched by women researchers than any other method, since its side effects and long-range effects are uncertain. The pill is 97-99 percent effective, and therefore doctors and health professionals are often very biased in its favor. Some medical personnel push the pill, and withhold information showing the pill may be harmful to some women, and some even hold the opinion that a woman is being irresponsible about birth control if she refuses to take the pill (especially after an abortion). No matter how clinically effective the pill may be, it will not be *actually* effective if women feel uncomfortable about taking it, and begin to "forget" a pill now and then. Even if a woman feels very good about taking the pill, she cannot use it for the duration of her fertile years. Some doctors recommend that a woman go off the pill every few years to allow her body time to function normally again. There is no way to be sure, since research in this area is still in its infancy, but it may be unwise to use the pill for more than 5-7 years total.

How does the pill work? The pill introduces small amounts of synthetic hormones into a woman's body which prevent the ovaries from releasing an egg. Therefore, without an egg to fertilize, pregnancy cannot occur. The pill's synthetic hormones, estrogen and progesterone, are naturally present in a woman's body in varying amounts throughout her menstrual cycle. Taking the pill induces a constant amount of estrogen into your system which simulates the condition of early pregnancy. There are different kinds of pills, all containing different amounts of estrogen and progesterone. It is safest for a woman to take the lowest dosage necessary to maintain effective contraception.

Possible side effects of the pill include: nausea, headaches, depression, water retention, weight gain or difficulty in losing weight, lethargy, blood clots, high blood pressure, aggravation of already existing cancer, increased vaginal infections, urinary tract infection, increased susceptibility to VD, breast swelling, lowered immunity to infectious diseases, increased oiliness of skin and scalp, gum inflammation, aggravation of existing epilepsy or asthma. A complete medical history should be taken before a woman is given the pill. If a woman is already suffering from any of the conditions mentioned above, the pill may aggravate it. Many women with health disorders should not take the pill.[37]

The pill is not for every woman, nor is it for any woman over an extended period of time. Each woman needs to be aware of all the risks and prepare herself with the facts before asking her doctor. You should be sure that the most significant health factors for your body and family history are weighed seriously against the advantages of the pill.

The pill is taken every day during a monthly cycle of 28 pills, or for a monthly cycle of 21 pills stopping for 7 days, then resuming the pill for another 21 days. If a pill is forgotten, two must be taken the next day. Skipping two or more pills is reason enough to use a backup method of birth control. A backup method should also be used when first starting to use the pill, and for the first month if you switch to a different brand of pills.

The clear advantage of the birth control pill is that a woman is free to enjoy sex spontaneously at any time without any preparations other than remembering to take it every day.

The *morning-after pill* is just what it sounds like. It is usually a five-day series of diethylstilbestrol (DES) which must be started within three days after unprotected intercourse. The rate of effectiveness is undetermined, since there is no way of knowing if fertilization had occurred or not, but it is known that its effectiveness decreases as the interval between the time you have unprotected intercourse and the time you start the pills increases. The most common side effect is severe nausea. Other side effects include headache, menstrual irregularities and breast tenderness. Women should watch out for symptoms of blood-clotting disorders: severe headaches, blurring or loss of vision, severe leg pains, chest pain, shortness of breath. The pills should be stopped immediately and the doctor contacted if any of these occur. This drug has been linked with the occurrence of vaginal and cervical cancer in the daughters of women who some years ago, had it prescribed for them during pregnancy, supposedly to prevent miscarriage.[38]

Menstrual Extractions circumvent the tension of late periods, the discomfort of regular periods, and the need for abortion by simply removing the menses at the time a normal period would begin. This procedure is being experimented with in advance self-help groups at a few women's centers. A few private physicians offer this service, but not many. The long-range effects of menstrual extraction are being studied by women in advanced self-help groups who know each other's bodies very well. There exists an atmosphere of trust as well as the intelligent use of the Del-M kit, which has a by-pass valve that prevents any air from entering the uterus. Some kits for menstrual "induction" have been devised by certain companies which do not have such a valve and are therefore very dangerous. Without the mutual caring and commitment of a group of women well versed in self-help techniques, menstrual extraction is very dangerous. Menstrual extraction is *not* an abortive technique, since pregnancy cannot be determined this early. The procedure should not be attempted by anyone who is not part of an advanced self-help group.

A word of caution: there are many newly established women's groups that are, unfortunately, not everything a woman's group should be. In fact, a poorly organized or unskilled self-help group could be as dangerous to your health as a bad doctor or clinic. When choosing a women's collective or group, check their reputation in the community and whether or not they meet health regulations. Make sure the professionals there are knowledgeable, and are willing to explain procedures and practices, and that they have a sense of professional pride. A good women's center will also be clean and pleasant.

NATURAL METHODS

Many women are turning to natural methods of birth control after trying existing mechanical and chemical methods and finding some objection to each one of them. Other women are using natural methods because of religious beliefs which leave them no other options. If we hold the philosophy that sex is good and natural in itself, then it only makes sense that there would be a natural, safe, and effective way to avoid unwanted pregnancies.

There are cultures which hold the belief that a woman will not get pregnant before marriage, even when enjoying sexual intercourse with many partners over an extended period of time. The Muria tribe in India believes that a woman can only become pregnant when she becomes mentally committed to a man and remains physically faithful to him. The young people of this culture grow up in a children's commune and they perform a special rite to the god of the "ghotul" to prevent a young woman from becoming pregnant. Only 4 percent of the Muria women do become pregnant before marriage which suggests that their mental form of birth control is highly effective. The Murias live in harmony with nature and each other. Sexuality is considered a powerful and natural energy and therefore given a place in daily life which allows its expression to be gentle and loving. Verrier Elwin, an English theologian, who lived with the Muria has written a book, *Kingdom of the Young*, which describes these people in great detail. Other books are listed in the bibliography and in Appendix I.

Unlike the Muria, we Americans do not universally agree that sex is inherently good and natural, or that a woman cannot get pregnant before marriage. On the contrary, we have very mixed feelings about sex and one of our long-lived myths is that pregnancy is a "just punishment" for premarital indulgence. I know of one case in which mental birth control has worked for a woman for seven years. I also know of many women who end up in abortion clinics because they "didn't concentrate hard enough." Extensive training in various mental disciplines is still no guarantee a woman will be able to control her fertility, especially if she has the slightest ambivalence about becoming pregnant.

It is probable that mental birth control works largely with women who grow up in a culture that believes in it, as the Muria tribe. People who try to incorporate beliefs into their lives that are not culturally consistent, generally meet with failure.

All systems of natural birth control require sexual abstinence during a woman's fertile time of month, and are concerned with determining exactly when this fertile time occurs. The method for discerning when ovulation takes place is the main variable that distinguishes one kind of natural birth control from another. Natural birth control involves more cooperation between a woman and man than other methods, as well as more time for learning the proper use of the chosen method. The advantages are that a couple can learn to express love and intimacy in other ways besides sexual intercourse, that a woman comes to know her body very well, and that a woman no longer need worry about negative side effects of birth control. The disadvantages are that improper understanding of any detail of any of the methods can lead to a pregnancy, that a woman who does not live in the same geographical area as her sexual partner may not be able to plan every visit to coincide with her safe period, and that as mentioned before, Masters and Johnson found there are some women who may spontaneously ovulate during intercourse. Unfortunately a woman only discovers this fact when she becomes pregnant.

The following methods of natural birth control seem to be the most effective and the most scientifically based.

The Ovulation Method was developed by Drs. Lyn and John Billings of Australia. They discovered that a woman's monthly cycle is reflected in her cervical mucus. Most of us have noticed variations in our mucus but weren't aware that there was a consistent pattern. The ovulation method requires that a woman diligently check her mucus symptoms daily and thereby learn when ovulation occurs. Complete abstinence for one month is required while a woman gets to know her own mucus pattern undisturbed by any other substances such as semen or contraceptive foam, jelly, or cream. Although the method is very simple and easy to learn there are many details involved that must be followed exactly. Learning this method from a trained teacher is advised. The Billings' emphasize the concept of "couple fertility" which gives the man an important role to play in the successful application of this birth control method. Abstinence is necessary during a certain time in every cycle. Each woman will have a different number of "safe days," which therefore requires a varying length of abstinence. Presently HEW is conducting a three-year research project on the Billings' method, which so far has been about 99½ percent effective (according to its proponents) when used very precisely. Whether some failures attributed to a mistake made by the users are actually pointing to some other reason for failure is not yet known. One woman in northern California reported failure due to taking antihistamines for a cold which also dried up her vaginal mucus and, therefore, she missed the warning that ovulation was near. Information on the Billings method can be obtained from any Catholic Archdiocese office since this method is sanctioned by the

Catholic Church. Happily, the ovulation method may prove to be one of the easiest and most effective methods of natural family planning.

Lunaception was discovered by Louise Lacey who became committed to finding a natural way to avoid conception after discovering she had developed lumps in her breast due to extended pill use and already knowing that other methods were not effective for her. She was unwilling to risk a second abortion, and therefore chose to be celibate and creative. The result of her search for an alternative choice is a new natural method of birth control which works for her and all the 29 women who have been documented as using it correctly in Lacey's book. Lunaception is based on the knowledge that our biological rhythms are often triggered by light which has a direct effect on our pineal gland, and that in primitive societies women's menstrual cycles were in synchrony with the moon's cycle: ovulation occurred at the full moon and menstruation at the new moon. Ms. Lacey read of Dr. Dewan's experiment which resulted in regularizing women's mentrual cycles. The women slept with a small light on during the 14th, 15th, 16th and usually the 17th nights of her menstrual cycle. Ovulation was triggered and the regularizing of the women's cycles resulted. (The menstrual flow follows from 9 to 16 days after ovulation.) Enthusiastic about this scientific verification, Louise set out to experiment on herself. All the details of Lunaception must be followed exactly for a woman to be protected from pregnancy. Reading Louise Lacey's book carefully is a must before trying her method. Lunaception not only worked for Louise Lacey but she discovered a much larger cosmic vision and a fuller feminine identity through her research. The distinct advantage of Lunaception is that it cuts down on the required length of abstinence from as many as 18 days to 4 days.

Sympto-Thermal and *Temperature* methods of natural birth control involve taking your temperature every day, at the same time each day. The hormonal changes occurring around ovulation result in a slight reduction in temperature just before ovulation and a slight rise in temperature afterward, which continues for about ten days. The temperature method involves only the charting of temperature changes. Unfortunately, this is not always reliable, since our temperatures can rise and fall due to the onset of a minor illness, infection, or other reason. The sympto-thermal method also includes the charting of a woman's vaginal mucus pattern, and is estimated to be a very effective method by Karen Faire Hammond, who has researched natural birth control methods for her master's thesis at California State College, Sonoma. Information on her pamphlet is included in the references. The pamphlet explains both theory and practice.

Astrological Birth Control was developed by Dr. Eugene Jonas of Czechoslavakia in the mid fifties. He wanted to find a natural method of controlling fertility that was consistent with his Catholic beliefs. Dr. Jonas' extensive study involved nearly 30,000 women. He found a correlation between the angle of the sun and moon at the time of her birth and her fertile period each lunar cycle. A woman is most fertile 24 hours preceding the time at which her sun-moon angle recurs. This fertile time can be at any time during a woman's menstrual cycle, which may well explain why so many women have conceived during their period. (The ovulation method also advises abstinence during the period but for other reasons.) Astrological birth control asks that a woman abstain during her mid-cycle ovulation time as well as her cosmic fertility time. The two may or may not coincide. This method gives no way of determining the mid-cycle ovulation so another method must be used for this. A Czech study involving 1,252 women and two American surveys involving a few hundred women have indicated an effectiveness rate of 97.7 percent. A full explanation of the dynamics of this method can be found in *Natural Birth Control* by Sheila Ostrander and Lynn Schroeder.

Combining two or more of the natural birth control methods can offer more peace of mind. If the most conservative measures for determining when ovulation is about to occur are used from each system, then reliability is enhanced. But so is the number of days you must abstain.) The sperm can live in fertile mucus for about two to five days. One experiment found a hardy little bugger alive and well after nine—but that is quite rare. An egg lives for 12 to 24 hours. You have to be *sure* no sperm are already present and waiting for the egg to be released. The same hormones that trigger ovulation also cause the cervical mucus to change from the "infertile" to "fertile" state and at the same time cause a slight variation in body temperature.

Abstinence from sexual intercourse is one sure way of avoiding pregnancy. Actually, it is the only method 100 percent effective.

Most women do not choose complete abstinence as their only form of birth control for very extended periods of time. However, many women are enjoying periodic abstinence as part of natural birth control or for its own growth. Freely chosen abstinence can give a woman time and energy for herself. Learning about our own physical and psychological rhythms apart from the stimulation and complexities of a sexual relationship can be rewarding. Taking time for one's own creative work may also precipitate a decision to be temporarily celibate. Some of the common feelings women experience during their celibacy is a greater appreciation for their own femininity, a deeper valuing of relationships with other women, which develop independence and self-affirmation. As one woman expressed it:

> I have been celibate over a year now and I have enjoyed my independence and freedom. My own creativity has blossomed since I put my own needs first now and at the same time my appreciation for others—men and women is so much greater. My feminine identity has developed strength and an expression which is uniquely my own. I have learned how to nurture myself and am now aware of what I want in a relationship with a man and know I do not need to settle for less. The emotional fullness I have developed gives me the clarity to enjoy what sharing is possible in each of my many and varied relationships. I feel ready for sexual intimacy again and have been preparing myself by studying natural birth control methods and charting my own cycles. Now that I know myself so much better physically, emotionally, and spiritually I know I will be able to choose a sexual partner who will only add joy to my life's journey.[39]

Just because more people are now accepting sex as natural it does not mean that everyone will desire sexual intimacy all of the time. We each have sexual rhythms which are important to respect. Likewise, a harmonious sexual relationship will involve integrating two such rhythms. Preventing unwanted pregnancies is a challenge sexual intimacy presents.

PERMANENT BIRTH CONTROL (STERILIZATION)

Our discussion on birth control methods would not be complete without mentioning sterilization. Many women and men who are sure they don't want any more children or any children at all are opting for permanent birth control through simple surgery.

Male sterilization is called a vasectomy. A vasectomy involves cutting and tying the tubes leading from the testicles to the penis. A sperm count must be done a few weeks later to insure no further sperm are present during ejaculation. This simple operation can be performed in a doctor's office under local anaesthesia. It is much easier and less expensive than female sterilization.

A hysterectomy is not necessary for effective female sterilization. The easiest method is the endoscopic technique in which the fallopian tubes are cut and cauterized so that the sperm can no longer reach the egg. A few days in the hospital is usually necessary. Both male and female sterilization are almost 100 percent effective. Most of the time these operations are irreversible. Sexual enjoyment is not impaired in any way. On the contrary, it seems most women and men enjoy sexual intercourse more after sterilization, since they are no longer worried about unplanned pregnancies. A good resource for sterilization information is Lawrence Lader's *Foolproof Birth Control—Male and Female Sterilization.*

BEYOND BIRTH CONTROL

Preventing abortion necessitates preventing the situations which lead to many unwanted pregnancies or rejected children later on. Some of these are rape, birth defects and a woman's ill health.

Rape victims represent a small proportion of the women seeking abortions, but most women who do become pregnant through rape will understandably choose abortion. Unfortunately, in our society men are taught to be sexually aggressive. A distorted expression of extreme frustration and hostility is rape, an insult to a woman, terrifying, and potentially physically and mentally damaging. Some of the ways a woman can prevent rape are to avoid being alone with a man that you don't trust, even if you know him and he is part of your family; to take a taxi or walk with friends after dark; to learn self defense techniques; to wear conservative and concealing clothing in areas of a city, rural community, or county where it is unusual for a woman to wear short dresses, low cut blouses, no bras, or anything else that may be regarded as "sexy." We are still living in a society filled with conflict, therefore, we need to take precautions to insure we don't become the victims of anyone else's hostility or pathology.

Birth defects strike 250,000 children born in the U.S. each year. (That's about 5-6 percent of the total number of births.) Nearly 25 percent of adult illnesses can be traced to genetic factors.[40] Recently, medical science has formulated new tests for detecting many genetic diseases while the fetus is still in utero. Only after 14–16 weeks of pregnancy can a woman have an amniocentesis, a procedure for removing some amniotic fluid through a needle inserted through the abdomen into the uterus. The extracted fluid contains enough fetal gene cells to determine through various laboratory tests if a suspected disease is present. Unfortunately, this procedure seems to increase the likelihood of miscarriage in one out of every 150-200 women who undergo it. The test results are not complete until one week to one month later. There seems little point in having the test unless a woman has good reason to suspect a damaged fetus and is willing to abort if she finds that is the case. If there is a history of genetic disease in the family a woman may prefer to submit to this procedure and take the chance of a late abortion rather than continuing the pregnancy and giving birth to a defective child. Genetic counseling prior to conception can be very helpful for couples who have histories of genetic disease. Complete medical histories of both partners' families are studied and often medical examinations are suggested for each. The results of the tests can indicate the degree of risk of producing a defective child. Sometimes there are preventive measures which can be taken prior to conception to reduce the risk. Your own physician can give you information on genetic counseling or you can write the National Genetics Foundation (see references).

One of the most common causes of birth defects is a woman catching German measles (Rubella) during the first three months of pregnancy. If you are not yet pregnant and not sure if you had the disease as a child (which makes you immune), you can be tested and immunized. Immunization must be obtained at least three months before you plan to become pregnant.

Down's Syndrome (or mongolism) occurs more frequently in babies born to women 40 years of age and older (2-3 percent of pregnancies). Some women in that age group prefer to have an amniocentesis done rather than take a chance. Some genetic diseases occur most frequently in certain racial groups such as Tay Sachs Disease, which mainly affects eastern European Jews; and Sickle Cell Anemia which is most prevalent among Blacks.

If a woman suffers from malnutrition during pregnancy, fetal brain development can be retarded. Healthy parents are more likely to produce healthy children. Teenagers may also risk delivering a child with birth defects simply because their bodies have not finished growing and are therefore not ready to nurture another life. More adolescent girls bear children in the United States than in any other Western developed nation; this is known to be one of the causes for our higher infant mortality rate.

The growing amount of pollutants in our environment may be another cause of birth defects. All children born in the United States today are likely to have traces of DDT, as well as other carcinogens in their body tissues. Much more research needs to be done. To maintain our quality of life, we are going to have to find alternatives to all of these dangerous substances.[41]

The National Foundation of the March of Dimes, which is dedicated to the prevention of birth defects, warns pregnant women not to take any non-prescribed medicine, including aspirin, sleeping pills, laxatives, and "fizzy" powders for stomach upset. Some prescribed medicines should also be carefully evaluated as to risk.

Women with certain physical illnesses should not become pregnant. Some women realize that their health is poor and will become worse after becoming pregnant. Severe heart, kidney, and diabetic conditions as well as cancer are some of the illnesses which most frequently are aggravated by pregnancy. Bearing too many children too quickly can also weaken a woman's health and stamina and make future pregnancies a threat to her well-being. Women whose health may be affected by pregnancy often seek sterilization to eliminate the mental anxiety that accompanies the threat of an unwanted pregnancy. The effect on a child should also be taken into account. A woman should not bear a child if she is not healthy enough to adequately care for a child, or if the child's health will automatically be hurt because of the mother's condition.

CHAPTER SEVEN

Young, Pregnant and Scared

All adolescents in our society, boys and girls alike, struggle with the problem of being physically mature while being expected to postpone the adult fulfillment of their sexual drives. Yet if the boy engages in sexual activity, his body does not change . . . For the girl, the consequences of sexual activity, regardless of the penalties society adds, are great, simply by virtue of the fact that she is a woman.

Gisela Konopka

IF YOU ARE EIGHTEEN years old or under, are pregnant, and don't want to be, you are not alone. You have the company of hundreds of thousands of young women who share your plight. Each year 300,000 young women choose abortion as their "way out" of an unplanned pregnancy. Many thousands more continue their pregnancies and either give their babies up for adoption or raise them with or without a husband. You may say that's all well and good but, "What am I going to do?" Chances are you are afraid or uncomfortable about telling your parents. If you feel okay about telling them, and feel they will help you, that's great! Ideally, every young adult should be able to share all the joys and problems of growing up with her or his parents. This is not always the case. Each young woman will have to decide if and when she wants to tell one parent or both. Some young women prefer to think about what they want to do about their pregnancy before they tell their parents. Others prefer to have an abortion, or leave town, have the baby, and tell their parents after it's all over. Often parents can be much more understanding and accepting than one would imagine they would be. Ideally, it would be great to know that your parents could be trusted to offer comfort and guidance at this time without insisting you accept what *they* want for you. If this is not the case, and you want to, or have to make your own choice, you may have to face this choice alone.

You may feel very self-conscious about being pregnant. No one can tell that you are just by looking at you, until about the fourth month. Although some mothers are very intuitive and seem to "know" everything, no one can be sure unless you say something. You may think people are staring at you and they must suspect you are pregnant. Almost every young pregnant woman experiences these feelings. You're seeing the world through your own anxiety, and assuming everyone can see inside you.

If you are sure you want an abortion, you are legally free to have one *without* the consent of your parents. How you are going to pay for the abortion and where you can go to get one is another matter. The first step is to have a pregnancy test. Review Chapter Three for details on pregnancy testing. Do not delay. Details on where to obtain an abortion are in Appendix II. As mentioned previously, the sooner you have your abortion, the less expensive and easier on your body it will be. First trimester abortions are in fact much easier on your young body than childbirth would be. Once you have written proof that you are pregnant, (a doctor who completed a pelvic on you must sign a note, the urine test results don't count) you can apply for medical assistance to have your abortion, even if your parents have money. This is called emergency medical care and is available through the Department of Social Welfare (at least in California).

In some areas of the country you will be meeting with greater resistance than others. Abortion is a controversial subject and many adults have strong opinions pro and con. Getting an abortion in the south or midwest, or a small town anywhere in the country may be difficult. All along the way you must be determined and resourceful if your choice is to abort. It is not easy encountering difficulties when you may be feeling upset or may have to be discreet about your search. This may be the first major decision you have to face alone.

It is even harder to get what you want in an environment that may not be supportive of your choice. Some of the people working for the agencies you will contact may be friendly and others may be abrupt or insulting. Their attitude may have nothing to do with you personally. They may be just having a bad day or may be unpleasant people. When you are feeling sensitive and vulnerable, people's comments can hurt more than usual.

It is important you seek out the kind of assistance that is going to be helpful to you and supportive of your choice. Feminist health collectives and women's centers are very helpful. If there are none in your area, try Planned Parenthood. Planned Parenthood also honors your right to privacy and will respect confidentiality. If you are in a small town and fear your parents will find out, then go to the library or local phone company and find the phone book for a larger town or city nearest you. Look in the yellow pages under "Prenatal care," or if there is no listing, look under "Clinics." Agencies will refer for abortions if they do not administer them. Referral sources are listed in the back of this book. Often a sympathetic teacher or counselor at school can help you find the information you need. I suggest you ask them to respect confidentiality *if* you do not want anyone to know. It is important to remember that you are okay and you have a right to decide what *you* want to do about this pregnancy, despite anyone's attitude toward you.

"What if I can't decide?" If you can't decide what you want to do, your pregnancy will continue beyond the point where an abortion is possible and nature will have decided for you. Ignoring your pregnancy will not make it go away. Late abortions performed between 16–24 weeks after the first day of your last menstrual period are dangerous, and should be avoided. If you are busy blaming yourself for getting pregnant in the first place you are wasting a lot of energy postponing your decision-making. Remember, if you simply go on "stewing in your own juice" your pregnancy will continue and soon your protruding stomach will tell the people you did not want to know. This is not the end of the world! Although common, fantasies of suicide, running away from home, and trying to abort by yourself are self-destructive and counterproductive to positive action. Do not try to abort yourself under any circumstances! You can severely damage your body. What to do? Be cool and start thinking.

"I can't think!" Sometimes strong feelings can get in the way of clear thinking. Almost every young woman who faces an un-

planned pregnancy feels scared and guilty. If you are not feeling guilty or scared, don't think you should. Sometimes feelings change very quickly—sadness, giddiness, fright, guilt, anger, numbness. Feelings are important. We can learn from our feelings. They can help us grow. But feelings can also overwhelm us and keep us from taking care of business. Allowing yourself time to release your negative feelings in a safe way, can be very helpful. If you feel like crying, find a place where no one will disturb you or find a friend who will just hold you and not ask you to stop. Just cry until you feel better. If you are angry, let yourself begin to beat a bed or pillow with your fists. Begin slowly at first, and then more quickly, and yell! (Be sure no one is around.) Say whatever you want to say. Let it out! When you are finished crying and/or screaming just lie down and feel the energy flowing through your body. Let yourself relax, or take a walk in a quiet place.

If you are feeling confused, try to separate the conflicting ideas that are spiralling in your head. You might want to write down all the different things that you feel and think. Explore your thoughts. Are all the thoughts your own, or are you hearing someone else's voice telling you what to do? If you feel certain views belong to someone else you know, then it may help to clarify your thoughts if you pretend that person is in a chair, and talk to her or him. Tell that person how you feel. Then sit in the chair and pretend you are the other person talking to you. Keep switching roles until you feel you clearly understand which thoughts are yours, which thoughts are the other person's, and how you both feel and think. You may not completely resolve the conflict but at least you may begin to trust your own feelings and be able to say "no, that's not what I really feel" when you hear others' words in your head.

After you feel more calm, here are some questions you can ask yourself to help you sort out and clarify your conflicting feelings:

• Am I happy about this pregnancy?
• Do I really want a child now?
• Will I be able to finish school if I have a child?
• Do I feel ready for all the responsibilities that are involved in childrearing?
• Do I love the father of this child? Does he love me?
• Do I want to marry him now? Does he want to marry me now?
• What are my plans, goals, and hopes for my own future? How does having a baby fit in with the kind of life I want to live?

- How do I imagine my parents would feel about me raising a child and the possibility of their supporting both of us for a few years?
- Do I want to raise a child alone if my circumstances make that a possibility?
- Do I want to have the baby and then give it away?
- Do I want to leave home and live elsewhere until the baby is born?
- Do I want to talk with someone before I decide?

Answering these questions may help you get a clearer idea about what your life may be like with a child. You may not be able to finish school, travel with friends, or develop your own skills in ways you had planned. You may increase your dependency on your parents just at a time when you were feeling the need for greater independence. You may choose to raise your child alone, rather than marry a man you do not love. If you marry the father of your child, this will be a big adjustment for you. No matter what you decide to do, the decision is yours, and you are the one who will have to live with it.

Even if you are worried that you will make the wrong decision, it is necessary to make *a* decision. *Not* to decide is to avoid responsibility. It is necessary, despite your fear, to find all the information you need to make an intelligent decision, and then act. Being pregnant and thus confronted with choices can be viewed as an opportunity to blossom into womanhood. Whether or not you decide to continue or terminate you pregnancy, you can view this as a tremendous opportunity to grow and to know yourself better.

Sometimes it helps to hear how someone else became pregnant and what she learned about herself because of it. She says:

> My upbringing was Catholic. I was taught that sex was holy inside marriage and altogether unholy anywhere else. My parents taught me nothing about sex in an open, honest way. The closest thing that came to sex education was a continuing series of lectures on "how boys only want one thing," "that boys take advantage of girls," and "we trust you because we know you won't do anything wrong."
>
> Their actions displayed a sizable portion of mistrust, and frankly I couldn't see what all the big deal was about anyway. I personally never felt that sex was bad. However, their message was clear—the worst thing I could ever do would be to get pregnant. In the process of establishing myself at a new university far away from home, (after

the painful ending of my first-love relationship) I began to assert my independence in new ways, and at the same time, attempted to heal my emotional wounds. I wanted to act on my feelings that sex was not bad and went to a doctor for birth control. He refused my request because I was a minor.

My early training of "sex is evil" turned into "I am evil" because I want to have sex. My feelings of self-worth were shaky due to the first-love relationship ending suddenly. My rational mind took a vacation. I felt confused and masochistic. Men in those days still looked down on women who agreed to share sex with them. Women, out of self-defense, didn't dare admit they had ever "done it." I felt alone, alienated. I began using foam to complement the old "pulling out" method. One day I spontaneously made love with a new man without foam. I had assumed that all men knew to pull out. I was wrong. I got pregnant.

It was only when I had actually become pregnant, that I realized that I had allowed my body to become the battle ground between the old mores of the past, which I was rejecting, and the new mores of my own making, which were frightening for me to strongly affirm all alone. My lack of self-affirmation sapped my strength to seek out another more cooperative gynecologist before it was too late.

To go to a gynecologist and say, "I want birth control," is to make the stand, "I want sex." I was not only taught that women are sexually passive, but also that to "commit a crime" unconsciously was far less despicable than consciously setting out to do so. I only hurt myself by not learning how to get what I wanted. Getting an abortion was certainly more of a hassle than going to another doctor for birth control. But I learned to value my life and my values through the experience and begin to stand up for myself a lot more. I know I didn't want to have a child until I had done something worthwhile with my life . . . after my abortion I began to make a lot of changes. When I do become a mother I will have a lot more to offer a child than I would have when I was younger.[42]

Sometimes we are taught that abortion is awful and we will regret it. That all depends on us. Often good things happen to us through an abortion. It is important to really face how our lives would be different if we had the child. It is interesting to listen to two women who had abortions in their teenage years:

How would your life have changed if you would have had your child?

• I couldn't have continued school. I couldn't have experienced the personal growth that I have. It's hard for me to imagine my life with a child. Only good things have come from my abortion. I have learned how to be alone and how to be alone within a relationship. I didn't know this before and I couldn't have had the space to find out if I had had the child.[43]

• Oh Jesus! God spare us! My life would bear no resemblance to what it is now. I would never have been able to finish undergraduate work, much less go to graduate school. I would probably have taken many more years to break away from the man who was my husband then, though I would have eventually. I might possibly have just given up and committed suicide, a form of escape I considered several times during that marriage. I would have been a rotten mother. Now I am happily married with a wanted child. My own growth has changed me deeply. Presently I lead psychodrama and encounter groups, and will be working with parents of battered children.[44]

These women and many others have used an emotional experience, such as their abortion, to grow and mature emotionally and psychologically. Having an abortion is not the end of the world, it may be a new beginning.

"I'm not pregnant after all!" Even if the pregnancy test results were negative, it is important to get birth control, or abstain. If your period does not come in a few more days, go and get another test. Remember the first test may have been taken too early to detect pregnancy. Sex is beautiful, but pregnancy scares are anxiety-producing and interfere with developing a relaxed and loving relationship. Most women now in their 20's and 30's admit to risking unwanted pregnancies during their early sexual experiences. Almost all of these women realize now what factors contributed to their risk taking attitudes. Some of these attitudes are: "Sometimes my mind was saying, 'Oh no, sex is wrong,' and my body was saying, 'This feels good'." "My body kept on having sex and my mind kept on blaming and promising that this would be the last time."

We sometimes feel pressured by our friends or a particular boy to "do it" and we give into the pressure. Often, when we are first exploring our sexuality, we feel the need for approval by men (or boys). Knowing that men notice you and find you attractive often feels good, but this means nothing in terms of your real worth. We need to affirm ourselves from within. Our worth can never be measured by the approval or disapproval of men or women.

If your feelings of self-worth rise and fall depending on how things are going with a boyfriend, then you have sold out to him.

We need to learn to enjoy ourselves and enjoy life no matter who is around or who is not. Now is the time to start finding out who *you* are and what you want. You may ask yourself if you really want sex now, or if other things really interest you more. You may fear losing all your friends or a particular boyfriend if you decide to stop "playing around." As we take the risk to be alone rather than to go along with the group, we learn that there will be new friends who have similar interests and values.

You might be very much in love with a young man. If he is truly your friend, he will want to share responsibility for sex and birth control. Planned Parenthood clinics offer special rap groups and classes for teenage women and men. If a young man will not share responsibility for birth control with you, you might question his sincerity as your friend; still, you'll have to take responsibility for protecting yourself from pregnancy.

Sometimes, young people who really love each other and want to get married fear their parents will discourage them because they are "too young." The temptation to risk a pregnancy may be great since this gives you a reason for "having to get married." More often than not, marriages agreed to for this reason fail, since motives of rebelling against parents and ongoing financial hardship interfere with love and nurturance. If you really want to get married, it is better to stand up for what you want, and avoid pregnancy until you are both ready to be parents.

"But I don't want an abortion!" That's fine too. Some young women who really believe that abortion is not a good thing choose to continue their pregnancy and give the baby up for adoption or raise the baby themselves. Although the issue of adoption and single motherhood were discussed in Chapter Four, there are special considerations for a young woman who chooses either of these routes. If you think you want to keep the baby, then your parents may have to become involved, because you and the baby will need help (unless you have a rich boyfriend who is willing to offer you lots of assistance). Some parents will resent this and others will be very understanding. It is important to think about how you can continue your schooling after the baby is born.

Whatever you decide to do with the baby you will have to decide how you are going to spend your pregnancy. Some schools suspend a young woman when she becomes visibly pregnant. Other schools have so many young women getting pregnant that they accept it. How will your parents feel about your living at home during your pregnancy? You may have already decided that you want to go away until the baby arrives. Maybe you are already away at school, or have a friend or sympathetic relative with whom you can live.

What if you can't stay at home and have no place else to go? If you are sure that you want to give birth and are having difficulty working out the details, you can go to a Birthright organization and they will refer you to agencies that can help you. Maybe you want to go to a maternity home. Many such places are not as dreary as they used to be and some of the staff can be very kind. No matter what the surroundings, you will at least be able to share a common experience with other young women like yourself. Some of these homes charge a fee, which may necessitate parental involvement. Often you can continue your schooling in such a home as well as participate in other activities.

Wage homes are private homes which trade room and board for housework and baby-sitting. Some families who open their homes in this way to young pregnant women do so out of a spirit of compassion; others do it for the free labor they receive. You should visit a home and be sure you feel comfortable about the situation before committing yourself. As with any business transaction, it is best to have the terms of the agreement clear at the beginning. Be sure you know how much work you are expected to do and that it will be an atmosphere in which you will be treated fairly and kindly. If you are old enough to have some personal savings you may choose to live on your own. Sometimes it is possible to find another young woman in the same situation who would like to share living expenses.

During your pregnancy, and afterwards if you keep the child, you will need to decide how you want to present yourself to the world. Denying your reality as to why you became pregnant, or where the child's father is, in order to "save face" in society is emotionally damaging to you. If you have a good attitude toward yourself, and carry yourself with respect and dignity, others will sense this.

Whether or not you decide to keep the baby, give up the baby, or to abort, you may want to talk with someone on a regular basis to resolve your feelings and get some feedback. A trained and sensitive counselor can be very helpful to help you decide and to help you with any unresolved conflicts after the fact. Sometimes, family therapy can help all family members sort out their feelings about your pregnancy. This can allow more honest communication and more realistic decision making for all concerned. Some good books on sex which have been written especially for teenagers are: Helen Southard's *Sex Before Twenty: New Answers for Youth; Sex Facts for Teenagers* by Evelyn Fiore and Richard S. Ward, M.D.; *Sex, Love and Birth Control: A Guide for the Young* by James E. Lieberman, M.D., and Ellen Peck.

After it's all over, you will have the rest of your life ahead of you. No matter what you did about this unplanned pregnancy, once you learn about birth control and your attitudes that precipitated this unplanned pregnancy, there is no need to repeat the same mistake.

CHAPTER EIGHT

Psychological
Consequences

*If we feel caged or trapped that cage is likely of our own mak-
ing . . . We are not the victims of internal aggressive or destructive drives which need to be controlled, but rather the
nurturance we find within ourselves can provide an environment in which we can all grow to full potential.*

Frances Clark

THROUGHOUT LIFE WE MEET SITUATIONS that demand we grow
beyond our present level of awareness. Depending on our perspective we call these situations problems or challenges. Every time we
face an undesirable event (like an unplanned pregnancy) in our
lives, consider the options, choose an option and act, we have affirmed our ability to take care of ourselves in the world. Most women find that having an abortion involves more than attending to
the practical details. The decision to abort is itself a statement that
a woman is freely opting to preserve the time and energy that
childrearing would demand for other activities (whether she is
married or single, or already has children or not). This activity
may simply be time for herself to contemplate, or such goal-orien-
ted activities as continuing school or a career.

In this chapter we will first consider all of the factors which
bear an impact on the psychological consequences of abortion. We
will then discuss the range of feelings which may occur and how to
deal with these effectively. Most women integrate their abortion
experience into the context of their lives and do not suffer long-

105

term effects. The decision itself is obviously not an easy one, and the integration process later on may take some time.

Social Context. There is a difference between an illegal abortion in which a woman may risk her life, health and reputation, and a legal abortion that is safe and legally sanctioned. The abortion trauma of days past was primarily created by the very illegality of the act. Any action that is legally and socially condemned is very upsetting to carry out—despite a person's own judgment that it is correct. Irene Claremont de Castillejo, a Jungian therapist, has addressed herself to this point:

> Now what is the effect of an abortion upon a modern civilized woman? For years I have been much concerned at noticing the disturbances caused by past abortions upon the minds of my women patients. I had thought that this was due to the abortion itself which I had assumed was contrary to women's psychological make-up. But recently I have become overwhelmingly convinced that the bad and lasting effect upon a woman is not the fact of the abortion itself, but is artificially induced by abortion laws. If my contention is correct that abortion has from time immemorial been part of women's lore, its possibility must be inherent in the deep layers of a woman's psyche.[45]

Today women are openly discussing their abortion experiences. According to a *Life* special report, Billie Jean King, the tennis champion, was the first woman to publicly admit having an abortion.[46] At last the social stigma is fading and with it the psychological trauma. Statistically, the aftermath of childbirth is now more likely to produce an upsetting psychological response than an abortion. Despite the general acceptance of abortion in the mass media and in large cities, a woman who finds herself vainly searching for a cooperative gynecologist in a small midwestern town is still likely to encounter anti-abortion attitudes and possibly even unkind remarks. Some geographical areas are steeped in a puritanical ethos that rejects abortion. A woman must be able to separate her own feelings about abortion from those society might try to impose on her.

The following account is from a woman who had two abortions. The first was an illegal abortion, the second, a legal abortion.

> Back in 1967 abortion was hardly spoken about in nice middle class families. When I became pregnant I hid myself away for nearly a month, totally numb, full of anxiety. Luckily my doctor mentioned a

clinic in Mexico that could help me. One friend whom I trusted went with me. After returning I dared not mention it to anyone. I felt very guilty, even though I knew I had done the best thing for me. Seven years later I again suffered from contraceptive failure. I had the second abortion right here in town. The women at the clinic were respectful of me. All of the women in the waiting room were friendly and giving each other support. I realized then that the big trauma I had gone through earlier had nothing to do with my own feelings about abortion, but had everything to do with the feeling that I was by law a criminal for wanting control over my own reproductive life.[47]

It is harmful to a woman's integrity to be forced into an abortion. No matter how accessible abortions may be, the decision to abort must be made by each individual taking into account their own needs and feelings. A woman who chooses an abortion unencumbered by outside pressures is least likely to suffer negative psychological after-effects. Martin Ekblad's post-abortion follow-up study of 479 Swedish women is frequently cited on this point. ". . . 65 percent of the women stated that they were satisfied with their abortion and had no self-reproaches; 10 percent had no self-reproaches but felt the operation itself was unpleasant; 14 percent had mild degree of self-reproach or regretted having had the operation." Ekblad also found that *the guilt was greatest in women influenced by others in favor of abortion and least in those who wanted an abortion themselves.*[48]

One woman whom I interviewed was forced by her family to have an abortion in the 1930s and it took her twenty years to recover from her fear of that experience. Many teenagers, especially, feel pressured by their parents to have abortions to "save the family's reputation." Teenage maternity is not easy on anyone involved, but the young woman herself is ultimately the one who must decide what to do. Do not let yourself be cajoled or intimidated into a abortion.

Some states liberalized their abortion laws prior to 1973 and advocated abortion if it was needed to preserve the physical and mental health of the woman. These laws often required a woman to obtain written endorsement from two or three psychiatrists verifying that the continuation of pregnancy would indeed present a physical or mental threat to the mother's health. Women who were mentally healthy often had to misrepresent their state of mind in order to qualify for an abortion. This undermined a woman's self-respect and integrity and demanded that she act weak and distraught in order to take care of her needs. Many women played the "poor me" game so well, they convinced themselves of their instability. Freedom of choice is the only honorable context in which a woman can assert her right to reproductive freedom.

If a woman has a loving and supportive relationship with her husband or lover, and especially if she has children already, her decision to have an abortion will be much easier. If she finds herself facing an abortion and realizing simultaneously that her husband or lover does not feel equal responsibility in this event and perhaps does not even support her emotionally (but becomes cold, angry, or leaves), this is bound to affect her psychologically. If the man does not really support her wish to have an abortion, but half-heartedly goes along with it because the woman wants it, this too can later affect her psychologically.

An abortion *can* bring a couple closer together. A committed couple who chooses abortion for health or financial reasons, or because they already have all the children they want can begin to nurture each other in new ways as a result of making this decision together. A man's response to a woman's pregnancy can determine whether the woman accepts or rejects her pregnancy; she may feel ready to have a child but may not be willing to raise a child alone. A man can love a woman very much and not want children, just as a woman can love a man and not want children. If the man is either not willing to give emotional or financial support for the child, does not feel ready for a child in his life, or is not willing to stay in the relationship, the realization that a woman is alone in her desire to bear a child may precipitate the ending of the relationship and/or the pregnancy. Facing two losses at once can compound sadness. If a man is not willing to share the cost of the abortion, or be emotionally supportive, it is obvious that he is not committed to the relationship. Although this is difficult to face, it is better to accept the situation and act accordingly. One woman shares her experience of this situation:

> We had talked about children, although neither of us planned to have them right away. The IUD failed and my love for D. naturally spilled over into a warm acceptance of the unplanned pregnancy. He be-

came suddenly aloof, and although was willing to listen to my feelings made it clear that he wanted nothing to do with a child nor with me if I continued the pregnancy. I felt very rejected and jolted into the awareness that my love had grown far deeper for him than his had for me. I couldn't bring a child into the world who had already been rejected by its father. I am glad I had the abortion, but it is painful to face the loss of the pregnancy and the loss of someone whom I loved. How could I continue seeing a man who felt so differently about our relationship?[49]

The opposite situation can also happen. A man may want his partner to continue with the pregnancy, and the woman is the one who would rather terminate it. How this can affect a man is discussed in Chapter Nine. A woman in this situation may find herself being hooked by feelings of guilt for her desire to abort and continue a career or pursue other interests besides childrearing. A couple will need to resolve this conflict. A woman who is not receiving support from her partner for her abortion is wise to find a friend or counselor who can be supportive of her. A woman's love for a man may not include the desire to bear his child, just as a man's love for a woman may not include a desire for children.

A woman's religious beliefs can be a very strong factor in the psychological consequences of her abortion. Many women who otherwise think abortion is the best choice for them may be plagued by guilt originating from their early religious training. The laws of every religion continue to be reinterpreted over the years to meet the needs of the time. Throughout history there have been individuals who have sought guidance for right action from within at times when their religious beliefs seem in direct opposition to the choice which seemed most right for them. Any woman seeking an abortion does so because she feels it is the best choice she can make in her circumstances. It may take a lot of long, serious thinking to come to a decision right for you. However, if a woman honestly believes she should or must act in accordance with the laws of her church, then she leaves herself no room for autonomous decision-making in areas which conflict with church teachings.

The social context in which we live always has some effect on us, whether or not a woman's peers and family accept her abortion (or even the concept of abortion), may have quite an effect on her psychologically. Negative judgments regarding abortion exist more in some parts of the country than in others. These negative attitudes can influence a woman to be uncertain of her choice or cause her to feel unnecessary guilt both before and after her abortion. If your environment does not approve of your decision concerning your pregnancy, you should try to deal with this, and possibly seek support and/or help in maintaining your affirmation of your choice.

Some cultures place more emphasis on the woman's role as wife and mother than others do. For a woman to decide not to have more children, or not to have any children within a cultural context that supports large families, can be just as difficult as for the single woman facing an abortion alone.

The actual abortion itself can have more influence on a woman's psychological response than any previous ideas, attitudes, or beliefs. Being prepared for the abortion is essential. A woman should know what to expect. In high quality clinics, women receive abortion counseling to familiarize them with all procedures and possible reactions in advance; having another woman there throughout the abortion to give support, alleviate fears, and to answer questions, certainly helps to avoid later psychological trauma. If a woman lives in a community where such care is unavailable, then she must be sure to *ask* what procedure will be used and what to expect. These questions and others are discussed in Chapter Two.

The attitudes of the doctor, nurse, and medical staff of the facility can have a very positive or negative influence on a woman during this sensitive time. Many facilities are staffed with compassionate professionals who wish they could give a woman more support than time allows. If an abortion counselor is not available, it is unrealistic to expect that all your emotional needs will be met. If you know that you have strong emotional feelings to work through concerning your abortion, it is wise to find either a good female counselor to talk with or a woman who has experienced an abortion. Sometimes just a close friend may help.

If a doctor or a facility is known for cold or judgmental attitudes, it is best to avoid such situations if at all possible. We deserve competent and compassionate care and we should take every step we can to insure this. Even a very stable woman who is sure of her decision can be upset by insensitive personnel. One woman who experienced this kind of insensitive treatment had this to say: "I didn't feel badly until I got to the hospital. All the nurses treated me as if I had done something awful, as though they really had more important duties than helping to take care of me."

Each woman's body responds differently to the abortion. Some women are not as sentitive to pain as others. Some doctors are more skilled in using techniques that will minimize pain than others. The longer a woman is pregnant, the more difficult the procedure becomes. Remember, first trimester abortions are much easier on the body (and maybe the psyche, too) than are second trimester abortions.

If a woman's life is generally unsettled, an abortion may be the event which gives her a "reason" for her unrest. The abortion itself may not be so much the *source* of the difficulty as the *symptom* of the difficulty. A woman may be distressed over being forced to make a major decision when she has not been accustomed to doing so.

Jean Baker Miller, M.D. in her book, *Toward a New Psychology of Women*, discusses the "paradoxical depression" which may follow a person's major advance toward taking on responsibility and self-direction in life: "Such depression may reflect the fact that the individual is forced to admit that he, himself, is responsible for what happens."[50] Choosing an abortion is a major step toward self-determination and may elicit depression in women who previously did not make conscious choices and accept responsibility and the consequences of them. In this case, depression, then, is not a result of the abortion per se but a symptom of a larger growth cycle the woman has initiated. The woman poet and potter, Mary Caroline Richards, in her book, *Centering in Pottery, Poetry, and the Person*, describes these growing pains:

> Symptoms of growth may look like breakdown or derangement; the more we are allowed by the love of others and by self-understanding to live through our derangement into the new arrangement, the luckier we are. It is unfortunate when our anxiety over what looks like personal confusion or dereliction blinds us to the forces of liberation at work. It takes courage to leave the nest of the tribe or the company and the coziness of "we happy few"; sometimes we have the good fortune to be pushed out, or to fall out.

Our psychological health is intimately related to our physical well-being. If we are suffering from vitamin deficiency, hormonal imbalance, or general fatigue, any major decision is going to be more difficult.

No matter what other factors may influence a woman before and after her abortion there are physiological influences at work. The hormonal levels which change just before a woman's period sometimes cause mental distress. This mental "haze" becomes even more pronounced in the first trimester of pregnancy due to the continued change of hormonal levels. Some of the confusion a woman feels in trying to "decide" may be a result of her physiological state than a result of the nature of the decision itself. Following abortion, the hormonal levels drop abruptly. About forty-eight hours after the operation a woman may begin to feel the effects of this phenomenon; depression, sadness and fatigue may result. If you experience this, it is important not to assume it is because you made the "wrong" choice. It is comforting to know that the imbalance is usually restored in a few days.

Individual women differ in their reaction to abortion. In general, however, women seem largely to be unharmed after the experience of an abortion. A recent study by Dr. Edmond Payne found that immediately preceding abortion, psychological stress was found to be very mild. In Dr. Payne's words, "These findings strongly support the impression that termination of pregnancy by induced abortion does not constitute a serious psychological trauma or precipitate prolonged emotional conflict for most women."[51]

Integrating Your Emotional Responses: Relief, loss, guilt, and anger are some of the emotions women experience after an abortion. Despite the probable influence of post-abortion hormonal changes, the intensity of feelings that each woman experiences can vary widely. In consciousness-raising groups, the impact of an abortion on a woman's life has been compared to anything from a major trauma to a tooth extraction. On the whole, as mentioned above, women do not suffer long-term effects. Just knowing the whole operation is over, that there is no more waiting, and that you are no longer pregnant is a relief. Sometimes the feeling of relief becomes so strong that you may feel like celebrating. Although you need to take it easy for a while, it is important to be good to yourself. There are no "shoulds" involved in how you should feel following your abortion. Relief may continue to be your dominant response, and that's fine. It doesn't mean you are a cold person or unfeminine. It simply means that a crisis in your life is over and you already are feeling energy to move on. There is no need to linger in negativity or impose any external code of behavior on yourself. Well-meaning friends can be overly concerned about you and you may begin to wonder if you shouldn't be more upset after all. It is important to be with someone after the abortion who can accept *however you may feel* and who will not impose his or her feelings on you. Relief is one of the many feelings you may experience. Your moods may swing, and this is also common.

Even if you are 100 percent confident that abortion was the best course of action for you, you may experience a sense of loss, uncertainty, or confusion after the fact. This does not mean you made an incorrect choice, maybe this feeling may be due in part to the hormonal changes mentioned above. It is possible this feeling is related to your allowing yourself to now experience the aspects of the situation which would have previously interfered with your taking action.

Sometimes an abortion can bring needs and desires to the surface you never knew were there. These feelings may be related to childbearing or may be related to relationships with men, your own mother, your self-worth, or your own unfulfilled expectations.

Guilt, a hoary emotional monster can drain us of energy, joy, and even the will to continue living. Sometimes it rears its ugly head when we least expect it. No matter how self-sufficient a woman is or how independent she thinks she is, most of us have been brought up in a social environment which scorned abortions. How many of us even heard the word mentioned in our childhood?

Guilt seems to be a socially conditioned emotion designed to serve as a self-corrective measure when a person acts contrary to the way she or he has been taught or to the way she or he believes he should have acted. If you listen carefully you may hear a parent or teacher's voice still resonating in the inner ear of your mind telling you what not to do, say, think, be.

It is important to evaluate whether or not you feel guilty because of parental or social attitudes you incorporate along your way or if you feel guilty because you feel your choice to abort was an error for you. In either case, learning from guilt and mistakes will help you grow and avoid risking another unwanted pregnancy. Letting go of guilt is not always easy. Just talking to women who have already worked through their guilt can be "healing." If you find it difficult to resolve your guilt feelings, maybe a professional counselor could help.

When we feel some injustice has befallen us, it is only natural to feel angry. An abortion can bring to the surface many realizations that were silently brewing in the mind's depths. Perhaps your birth control method failed and you feel wronged by medical science. Perhaps your partner has walked out or is unsupportive.

Understanding and exploring your conflicting feelings and emotions that may arise after an abortion can help you come to terms with them. An excellent book on getting in touch with your feelings is *Getting Clear, Body Work for Women* by Anne Kent Rush.

Consequences for Women in General: The three-year-old Supreme Court ruling on abortion has its psychological consequences for women who have never had an abortion. There is some evidence that knowledge of abortion availability influences some women to take more contraceptive chances. "Well, if I get pregnant, I can always have an abortion" is a statement which is heard more frequently these days. Some opponents of a woman's right to choose, believe this to be verification that legalization of abortion leads to more frequent abortions. The slight increase in contraceptive risk-taking resulting from the availability of abortion is negligible compared to the positive effects legalization has had: the large scale reduction in mortality rates and psychological trauma, and the rights a woman has regained over her own body.

More significant is the growing feeling among men and women that only wanted children should be brought into the world, and they now have the means to insure this. Knowing an abortion is available leaves her with no excuse to continue an "unwanted" pregnancy. Women are now able to free themselves of identifying with the traditional concept of the maternal role and expand their horizons to include other feminine roles—other avenues of self-development.

CHAPTER NINE

The Man Who Cares

In counseling the partners of abortion patients I have found that men do care. We feel that pregnancy is equal responsibility and men have been left out.

Randy Hollingshead

JUST AS EACH WOMAN'S RESPONSE to her abortion is unique, so also is the response of the man involved. This chapter will be primarily addressed to the man himself.

Many men are relieved to find that the abortion facility looks like a normal clinic or doctor's office. Images of back-alley abortionists may still come to mind and can color anyone's feelings about the procedure. Most abortion counseling is aimed at the woman, and you may spend a few uneasy hours waiting and wondering what is going on behind the closed doors. A woman may not know herself what to expect until just prior to the procedure, or may not feel like talking about it before it happens. Reading the following may help you understand some of the possible post-abortion reactions a woman may have, and how you can be of emotional support to her and help her with aftercare instructions.

Although you do not have to confront the actual physiological discomfort and adjustments a woman faces, the abortion may affect you just as deeply. Some men are so aware of their equal involvement in creating a pregnancy that they feel very left out and helpless when they can't *do* something to share in the termination of that pregnancy. One man, who felt guilty because his partner was the one who had to endure all the pain, said: "I wished I could have laid down next to her and shared in her pain as I had shared

115

in the pleasure. It was so hard to stand by and just wait, and know she was in there all alone and there was nothing I could do to help."[52] Another man said: "I would have preferred that I was pregnant and that she wasn't."[53] During my interviews, I heard many such accounts from men. This certainly emphasizes the fact that men are not necessarily cold and unfeeling at the time of an abortion.

An unwanted pregnancy is a crisis, and although each of us have our unique way of meeting such events, men have been socially conditioned to be the "strong" ones at such times. Your feelings may run very deep, and you may not feel strong at all, but maybe you feel you must act that way to give support to the woman. Perhaps you have your own conflicts about the abortion or possible fatherhood, your own feelings about contraceptive failure or your part in not using protection. If you keep all your feelings inside and refuse to share them, your partner may think that you do not care; this will probably disturb her very deeply.

Some women make their decision about their pregnancy without discussing it with their partners. They simply announce decisively, "I'm pregnant and I'm having an abortion." Some couples make decisions together, so if your partner doesn't include you, you may feel as if your opinions don't count. A woman may feel distant from you at this time because she knows it is her body alone that houses the pregnancy and must endure its termination. Although the decision to abort rests ultimately with the woman, you have a right to express how you feel about that decision. If you both have conflicting views, she may wish to avoid facing the conflict and decide to take care of the matter herself, leaving you feeling rejected or ignored. Try to understand that although you are a partner in the sexual love which resulted in pregnancy, it is the woman who is constantly aware of the situation—it is a total and constant body experience. For you, awareness of the pregnancy is not grounded in your own body experience, but rather in your caring for your partner.

Although you may love each other deeply, one or the other of you may feel unprepared or unwilling to have a child. This lack of agreement may precipitate a major crisis in your relationship. The most helpful thing you can do is achieve a balance between admitting your own honest feelings while giving your partner as much love, and support in her decision as you are able to give. Even though this decision may be difficult for you, remember it is the woman whose body is going through the hormonal and physiological changes, and it is her body that will go through the pain or discomfort involved; and it is she who is more intimately involved.

If you are both yet undecided as to what your final decision will be, it may be helpful to share your honest responses to the pregnancy itself; to share the projections you each have about how your relationship will change if you have a child, or how you feel about choosing an abortion. You must share and discuss your feelings and weigh the possible outcomes of each alternative.

Sometimes a woman experiences strong emotions at this time. Perhaps some deep resentments or fears concerning your relationship will surface. Perhaps your partner will realize painful aspects about her childhood or herself at this time. No matter how confused you may both become, it is vital to keep the lines of communication open and remain receptive to each other until a decision is reached as to your future involvement and the pregnancy.

Prior to the pregnancy, maybe your relationship was going through rough times, and you were both uncertain as to how long you would continue together. If you had decided to terminate the relationship, or have serious doubts about each other as a stable couple, an abortion, single parenting, or adoption may be the alternative.

Perhaps the pregnancy is precipitating a permanent split. If a woman feels ready and willing to have a child with a man, and he does not want a child at that time, it is often difficult for her to continue as lovers with him. The woman may feel her emotional commitment to their relationship is greater than his, and therefore it is unfair and dishonest for her to continue the relationship. The reverse is true as well. Sometimes the man is the one ready for childrearing and the woman is not ready for a child at that time.

One man who wanted his partner to continue the pregnancy voiced his thoughts this way:

> I really wanted this baby to happen. I loved R. and was ready to be a father and raise a family. It was difficult for me to understand that she wanted to become a doctor more than be the mother of my child. I couldn't accept the abortion and continued to protest up to the last minute in the doctor's office. As it turns out R.'s ambitions in life demanded a lifestyle I couldn't feel comfortable with, and I didn't want

to see that before. We eventually split up and it sure would have been harder if I had really succeeded in persuading her to have the child.[54]

No matter which side you find yourself on, the most helpful thing you can do for both of you is to express your feelings honestly and accept the outcome. This is the only basis for a worthwhile and lasting relationship. As one man said, "the truth about the situation saved both us from future regret."

Often during a crisis a couple can develop unhealthy ways of interacting. A woman may simply need nurturance and support. You can give this just by being there, holding her, and listening to her. The abortion can, however, bring a couple that is already close even closer through the caring, love, and mutual support that is expressed.

A woman who knows that an abortion is the best choice for her may want to explore the fantasy "Wouldn't it be nice if things were different and we could have the child?" This might scare you and may seem inconsistent with her decision to abort. We often make choices in life that are based on circumstances we wish we could change, but know we can't (at least not at the moment). Sometimes a woman needs to explore the possibility of motherhood at this time, even though she knows that she will discontinue the pregnancy. If you feel in touch with your own feelings about "how nice it would be if we could have this child," a woman will feel a lot more at ease sharing her fantasies with you. Even if you do not feel that way, it is helpful to remember that even unplanned and unwanted pregnancies may be experienced as pleasurable during certain moments.

Major life decisions are commonly made with accompanying uncertainty. Whenever we take a new job, move to a new town, start or quit school, we may not be completely certain that we did the right thing until after the fact. If a decision is unpleasant (as the decision to abort often is) our tendency is to make the arrangements, go through with our choice, and consider feelings afterwards. You may find that you and/or your partner just want to "get it over with" and neither of you want to talk about it. Perhaps the circumstances which weigh against continuing this pregnancy are so evident to both of you that there seems to be nothing to talk about, yet, it may still help you both to share your feelings with each other. Difficult choices which are inevitable can still be sources of profound growth if we allow ourselves to explore the meaning of the event for us.

Some women do not want to talk about the abortion immediately afterwards, but would rather forget the whole thing. If your partner feels this way, it is advisable to just allow her time to herself, but let her know you care and that you are there to listen if and when she wants to talk. Other women really want to talk afterwards, and find this opportunity a great relief. To just be there and listen is a very clear statement of your concern.

The emotions which can follow an abortion have been discussed in Chapter Eight and you can expect any or all of these from your partner. Many women experience the need to readjust as the hormone levels return to normal. This can cause moodiness. A few women change their mind at the last minute and decide not to go through with the operation, or go through with it and suddenly feel deep remorse. Although this rarely happens, it is important for you to be ready for the possibility. Most women simply feel relieved afterwards, but emotional reactions can unexpectedly surface later on. No matter when a woman (or a man) realizes that there is still unfinished emotional business remaining from a past abortion, it is important to take time out to understand its nuances. Any life situation can become a turning point toward greater self-fulfillment. Every difficult situation, in order to be integrated, and not repeated must be fully understood.

Since the advent of the pill, many men assume that all women are on it. This is not true, and it is becoming less common as women are abandoning the pill for health reasons or because of long-term use. In the 1950s, it was the man who bore the brunt of an unwanted pregnancy, "He knocked her up." A man was expected to use condoms. Now a man expects the woman to use something and most men do not ask to make sure. Paternity suits are no longer fashionable (though still exist), so the consequences of pregnancy for a man are not as threatening as they once were. We all grew up seeing romantic movies with passionate love scenes in which not a single gorgeous male ever stops and asks, "What are we using for birth control?" nor does any voluptuous female ever abruptly halt foreplay with, "Wait a minute, I've got to put my diaphragm in." Some human sexuality courses meet all semester, and somehow fail to mention birth control once. However, more and more classes are incorporating this need now.

For obvious reasons, birth control education is traditionally aimed at the woman. It is also apparent that the man's attitude and cooperation plays a large part in whether a woman uses her method consistently and correctly. A man is equally involved in every pregnancy, and therefore shares equal responsibility. If every man and woman practiced birth control, there would be no unwanted pregnancies, (except for those caused by contraceptive failure). Do not feel uncomfortable about bringing up the subject of birth control. Most women are delighted when a man asks her what method she is using and feels she is being respected and cared for.

A man can participate equally in some birth control methods like the condom and foam combination. If the diaphragm and jelly is used, the man can help apply the jelly and even learn how to insert the diaphragm as part of foreplay. If a woman uses the IUD, the man can check to be sure the string is in place every week by looking into the vagina with a flashlight after the woman has inserted her speculum. One man discovered that taking his vitamin pill at the same time each day the woman took her birth control pill helped her remember. Natural birth control methods require that the man be equally involved in creating loving alternatives to intercourse during the unsafe days; these methods even speak of couple fertility to emphasize the fact that "it takes two." Planned Parenthood clinics offer regular classes in birth control for both men and women. Soon the male counselors at the Special Care Center (mentioned below) will be writing birth control pamphlets addressed to men. See Appendix II for further information.

The Special Care Center is the only facility in the San Francisco Bay Area (or anywhere I know of) that offers a special group counseling session for the partners of women abortion patients. From 10 AM to 12 NOON on Saturday morning, while the women are being privately counseled, prepared for surgery, operated on, and recovering, the men learn about what is taking place from two male counselors. The abortion procedure is explained, as are the risks, complications, and aftercare rules. The men have an opportunity to air their feelings and concerns. Each man learns very quickly that he is not the only one who feels uneasy, or has false information or expectations. With accurate knowledge about what a woman is experiencing, it becomes a lot easier to know how to be supportive. The men in this group have a chance to talk about how the decision was made; in this way, they can become aware of any lingering conflict, and perhaps explore how to resolve this with their partners later on.

Birth control is discussed at length, and the men become well-acquainted with the various methods and how they can participate in using each one. The men who choose to come to the counseling sessions care very deeply for their partners and 50-80 percent of all the women's partners do attend this men's clinic. The women treated have a choice as to whether the man is even informed about the session or not. Most women do tell their partner, especially if there is an ongoing relationship between them at that time.

The need for men's abortion counseling grew from the awareness that most pregnancy counseling which invites the woman's partner to participate, focuses primarily on the woman; this has been considered only natural. A man's group not only creates a forum for sharing information, but it gives men a chance to receive emotional support during this crisis. Hopefully, every man going through an abortion with his partner will have at least a close male friend who can care enough and understand enough to just be there if men's abortion counseling is not available.

Men's abortion counseling is helpful to both men and women. Being more aware of the experience a woman is going through, helping with the aftercare instructions, and the fact that a man cares enough to share this experience with a woman will be emotionally as well as physically supportive to her. At the same time, involvement in abortion counseling enables a man to feel he is able to take part in the experience to some extent, and share the burden of this experience.

It would be helpful if men would suggest to abortion clinic personnel that such a group counseling service would be helpful. Many times an agency has never thought of this obvious need. Calling their attention to it and mentioning that this service does exist at the Special Care Center in Oakland, California may inspire more clinics to offer this valuable service to men and women.

Afterword

One warm, fragrant spring evening in 1969 found me sitting in an abortionist's office. The crisis of my unplanned pregnancy awakened me to my womanhood. I shuddered to think that my body could give birth to another before I had given birth to myself. A vision of the woman I wanted to become and the world I wanted to help create erupted before my mind's eye. I had no knowledge of my "herstory"—the contributions women had made to civilization throughout time. I knew of only a very few women who had distinguished themselves. The image of Isadora Duncan vowing to never marry resonated with me as I vowed to actualize my own gifts and talents, to find my own center, and to contribute meaningfully to creating a more loving world *before* I gave birth to a child.

For me, abortion has been a personal symbol of my awakening to the challenge of realizing my individual potential.

Eight years ago I never dreamed that I was one woman among thousands who were also awakening to the challenge of self-actualization. Although not every woman experiences a conflict between motherhood and self-actualization, many of us do—at least during some phase of our development. Now that abortion is legal, each woman knows she has the freedom to reproduce *only* when and if she chooses. I regard the legalization of abortion as a result of many women's collective vision of themselves as deserving the power to decide their own reproductive destiny.

What impact has legalized abortion had on women, their relationships to men and family, on society? Each woman may now plan her personal and professional life with the assurance that an unplanned pregnancy may be terminated if she chooses. More women may opt for long-term professional training or more mobile lifestyles. Women may begin to question more than ever their desire to have children. The motives, costs, and benefits of childrearing may be considered more thoroughly. If motherhood is no longer an inevitability and must be chosen, a woman will be far more likely to consciously plan childbirth/rearing to blend harmoniously into her life. When pregnancy and childbirth are consciously and freely chosen, motherhood is more likely to be one of the most fulfilling experiences in a woman's life. Knowing they have the choice, more women may opt to remain non-parents and realize they wish to devote all their time and energy to professional or creative expression. Women need no longer feel victimized by their reproductive organs, nor are they able to use childbearing as an excuse for not realizing their own visions for individual growth. Knowing abortion is available may increase contraceptive risk-taking by some, but in the long-run, the same self-affirmation among women which made the legalization of abortion possible will also influence the improvement of birth control education and the concept of self-help, and will engender a stronger tendency towards preventing unplanned pregnancies.

A woman who is assured that she need not bear a child unless she wants to is more likely to envision the best possible circumstances for childrearing. A woman who is devoting time and energy to her own self-development may also want the father of her child to devote time and energy to that child's upbringing. This has a very positive value. Men who have been traditionally cultured to develop themselves, but who have not been trained in the art of child nurturance will have the opportunity to develop qualities of patience, gentleness, and receptivity. Many men enjoy the chance to develop their own gentler side in this way and welcome the experience of staying home with their children. Parents who are leading fulfilling lives are able to nurture their child with their own fullness and more readily inspire a child to develop her/his own potential. In my experience, a child reared by parents who equally share in the responsibilities of home life develops in a far more balanced manner. Such a child experiences "Mommy" and "Daddy" as independent persons as well as sources for her/his nurturance which gives a child a non-sexist model for her/his own development.

Society will benefit from legalized abortions. Fewer unwanted children will be born. The unwanted child is least likely to receive the nurturance essential to becoming a healthy, happy adult and more likely to suffer from emotional instability or develop criminal tendencies. The negative results of enforced pregnancy is eliminated by legalized abortion. The positive aspect of legal abortion is that women who choose to be mothers will assume that role with a more positive attitude. Wanted children are more likely to enjoy a more harmonious upbringing and are more likely to mature into responsible citizens. Furthermore, the parent-child relationship is the most essential in the acculturation process; therefore the parental roles deserve a dignity equal to any of the most well-respected roles in society.

Perhaps it is not coincidence that as women won the right to terminate unwanted pregnancies, we simultaneously rediscovered the joy and fulfillment of childbirth/rearing. Women are affirming not only their physical femininity but also their "feminine consciousness." Although the first waves of the "woman's movement" focused on securing a woman's right to function in society on an equal footing with men, presently there is a new vision being brought forth—one in which society is infused with the qualities of "feminine consciousness." In the history of western civilization, the qualities of "feminine consciousness" such as physical nurturance, affection, intuition, emotional expressiveness have been primarily approved for women in the role of mother. Whether it is a result of socialization or whether there is some neurophysiological basis, most women are keenly aware of the needs of others and are willing to give time and energy to fulfill these needs. As we move into the many professions which were traditionally preserved for men, we need not function as a man, but we have the option of redefining our role and perhaps even our profession to include our femaleness.

We are now facing the simultaneous challenge of creating our own lives while we recreate our society. We have much to learn from the resources available through male-defined institutions and techniques. However, we have much to contribute as well. The first step is to become aware of our own experience of the world, to be true to our own selves.

Continuing the dance of our liberation requires finding a form to express our experience through. Our form can be art, science, business, medicine, education, and/or homemaking-childrearing. We are in the process of bringing forth a vision of wholeness, a society that will reflect the harmony of the feminine and masculine within each of us.

The legalization of abortion is but one of many important factors that is enhancing the ability of each woman to contribute her share in the ways that she chooses. I hope this book will be of value to women not only in the process of choosing what course of action to take with an unplanned pregnancy, but also will be of value to women in the continual process of giving birth to themselves.

Notes

1. Doe v. Bolton, 410 U.S. 179, [1973].
2. Rowe v. Wade, 410 U.S. 113, [1973].
3. Rowe v. Wade, 410 U.S. 113, [1973].
4. Rowe v. Wade, 410 U.S. 113, [1973].
5. Rowe v. Wade, 410 U.S. 113, [1973].
6. Rowe v. Wade, 410 U.S. 113, [1973].
7. Rosoff, Jeannie I., *Planned Parenthood—World Population Washington Memo.* July 2, 1976.
8. United States Commission on Civil Rights, *Constitutional Aspects of the Right to Limit Childbearing.* April 1975, p. 77.
9. Kimmey, Jimmye, *Legal Abortion, A Speaker's Notebook.* New York: Association for the Study of Abortion, Inc.
10. Sanger, Margaret, *My Fight for Birth Control.* Pergamon Press.
11. American Friends Service Committee, *Who Shall Live? Man's Control Over Birth and Death.* New York: Hill and Wang, 1970.
12. Means, C. in *Abortion: Law, Choice, and Morality* by Daniel Callahan. Grand Rapids, MI: Williams B. Eerdmans, 1972, p. 384.
13. Gilbert, Margaret Shea, *Biography of the Unborn.* New York: Hafner Publishing Company, 1962.
14. American Friends Service Committee, *Who Shall Live? Man's Control Over Birth and Death.* New York: Hill and Wang, 1970, p. 98.
15. *Ibid.* p. 96.
16. *Ibid.* p. 98.
17. *Ibid.* p. 64.
18. *Population Reports.* Vol. 5, Sept. 1976, p. 7–19.
19. "Digest: Find D & E is Safest Method of Midtrimester Abortion, but Saline is Less Risky than Prostaglandins: JPSA," *Family Planning Perspectives.* Vol. 8, no. 6, Dec. 1976, p. 275–276.
20. Richardson, John A. and Geoffrey Dixon, *British Medical Journal.* 1(6021), May 29, 1976, p. 1303–1304.
21. Excerpt from a letter written by a single woman in her early twenties.
22. Woolley, Persia, *Creative Survival for Single Mothers.* Millbrae, CA: Celestial Arts, 1975.

23. Hardin, Garrett, *Mandatory Motherhood*. Boston: Beacon Press, 1974.
24. Kimmey, Jimmye, *Legal Abortion, A Speaker's Notebook*. New York: Association for the Study of Abortion, Inc.
25. Wallerstein, Judith, *et al*, "Psychosocial Sequelae of Therapeutic Abortion in Young Unmarried Women," *Archives of General Psychiatry*. Vol. 27, Dec. 1972, p. 828–832.
26. Luker, Kristen, *Taking Chances: Abortion and the Decision Not to Contracept*. Berkeley, CA: University of California Press, 1975.
27. Erlich, Paul, "The Population Explosion: Facts and Fiction," *Sierra Club Bulletin*. Oct. 1968.
28. Luker, Kristen, *Taking Chances: Abortion and the Decision Not to Contracept*. Berkeley, CA: University of California Press, 1975.
29. Kimmey, Jimmye, *Legal Abortion, A Speaker's Notebook*. New York: Association for the Study of Abortion, Inc.
30. Summerhill, Louise, *The Story of Birthright, The Alternative to Abortion*. Kenosha, WI: Prow Books, 1973, p. 69.
31. Interview with mother of a preschool child, Berkeley, CA.
32. Rollin, Betty, *Motherhood, Who Needs It?* National Organization for Non-Parents, 806 Reistertown Rd., Baltimore, MD 21208.
33. *Ibid.*
34. Interview with single woman, late twenties.
35. Interview with married professional woman, mid-thirties.
36. Interview with male college student, early twenties.
37. Boston Women's Health Collective, *Our Bodies, Ourselves*. New York: Simon and Schuster, 1976.
38. Mills, Don Harper, "Prenatal Diethylstibestrol and Vaginal Cancer in Offspring," *Journal of the American Medical Association*. Vol. 229, No. 4, (July 22, 1974), p. 471–472.
39. Excerpt from journal of woman writer, early thirties.
40. National Genetics Foundation pamphlet. 250 W. 57th Street, New York, New York 10019.
41. Epstein, Samuel, "Birth Defects and Their Environmental Causes," *Medical World News*. McGraw-Hill, January 22, 1971.
42. Interview with woman artist, late twenties, single.
43. Interview with woman psychologist, late thirties.

44. Interview with woman therapist, early thirties.
45. Castillejo, Irene Claremont de, *Knowing Woman.* New York: Putnam, 1973, p. 94–95.
46. "Remarkable American Woman 1776–1976," *Life* special report, p. 61.
47. Interview with woman teacher, mid-twenties.
48. Ekblad, Martin, "Induced Abortion on Psychiatric Grounds: A Followup Study of 479 Women," *Acta Psychiatrica et Neurologia Scandinavica.* Supplement 99, 1955.
49. Interview with female graduate student, early twenties.
50. Miller, Jean Baker, *Toward a New Psychology of Women.* Boston: Beacon Press, 1976.
51. Payne, Edmond, *et al,* "Psychological Effects of Therapeutic Abortion," *Archives of General Psychiatry.* Vol. 33, June 1976, p. 725–733.
52. Interview with male teacher, early twenties.
53. Interview with male student, late teens.
54. Interview with male graduate student, UC Berkeley, early twenties.

Appendix I

LEGAL AND POLITICAL ACTION

If you are interested in taking legal action against some state law or public hospital which has obstructed your right to choose abortion the following groups should be helpful.

American Civil Liberties Union
22 East 40th St.
New York, N.Y. 10016
or
814 Mission St.
San Francisco, Cal 94103

National Organization For Women
San Francisco Chapter
415-398-6312
Consult your directory for the local branch nearest you.

The following organizations are good resources if you wish to direct time and energy into political action aimed at repealing old anti-abortion laws and preventing the passage of new ones which are presently being considered.

National Abortion Rights
   Action League
250 W. 57th St.
New York, N.Y. 10019

Women's Political Caucus
1921 Pennsylvania Ave. N.W.
Suite 300
Washington D.C. 20006

Women's Lobby
1345 G St. S.E.
Washington D.C.

Relgious Coalition for Abortion Rights
100 Maryland Ave. N.E.
Washington, D.C. 20002

Association for the Study of
   Abortion
120 W. 57th St.
New York, N.Y. 10019
(Tax-exempt source for information and reprints, also
current newsletter.)

Zero Population Growth
1346 Connecticut Ave., N.W.
Washington D.C. 20036

American Civil Liberties
   Union
(same as above)

Appendix II

The following clinics offer abortion as one of their services at reasonable rates and also offer good counseling.

Women's Choice Clinic
2930 McClure St. Suite 201
Oakland, Cal. 94609
415-444-5676

Buena Vista Women's Services
2000 Van Ness Ave.
San Francisco, Cal.
415-771-5000

Planned Parenthood
482 W. MacArthur Blvd.
Oakland, Cal.
415-654-3213
(Consult your local telephone directory for the Planned Parenthood in your area.)

Pregnancy Consultation
Center
4000 Webster
Oakland, Cal.
415-658-6660
(This clinic provides counseling for men by male counselors, as well as individual counseling for women. Vacuum aspiration performed till 14-15 weeks LMP.)

The following agencies are dependable sources for abortion referrals. Do not pay a fee to a profiteering referral agency for the same information which these organizations give for free.

Family Planning Referral
Service
800-772-2444 (no charge to calling party)

National Organization for
Women

Planned Parenthood or
Family Planning

Berkeley Women's Health
Collective
2908 Ellsworth
Berkeley, Cal.
415-843-6194

Clergy Consultation Services
(Be careful—sometimes these groups are reactionary.)

Abortion Clinic Directory
(Lists clinics in each state)

American Civil Liberties
Union Foundation
22 E. 40th St.
New York, N.Y. 10016
(50¢ each)

Appendix III

STARTING A WOMAN'S HEALTH COLLECTIVE

Some women have organized themselves to provide health care services for women simply because they were not receiving adequate care in their communities. A woman's health collective is a creative alternative to existing medical care. Funds are necessary to rent a facility, buy equipment, print literature. The first step is to start a self-help group which can meet in a woman's home. Knowledge is an important basis for effective action. Advance self-help groups often become committed to the project of organizing a collective which can serve the needs of many women in the community. Skills such as fund raising and grant proposal writing are helpful. If one or more women are interested in training at a women's health collective that is already functioning this can always be arranged and is an excellent way to learn the ropes. It's good to start small at first, perhaps as a special service of a free clinic which meets only once a week. The collective will naturally grow as more women benefit from the services and become interested in sharing this with other women.

Abortion referrals is a basic service to offer which can also result in developing bargaining power with facilites resulting in better treatment and lower fees. As the collective grows and expands abortions can eventually be performed at the collective which can then hire its own doctor who is cooperative, sensitive and highly skilled. Below is a partial list of women's health collectives throughout the country. Write the L.A. branch to find out if a new health collective has opened recently near you.

L.A. Feminist Women's Health
  Collective
1112 Crenshaw Blvd.
Los Angeles, Cal. 90019
213–936–6293

Ames FWHC
619 7th St.
Ames, Iowa 50010
515–232–9078

Oakland FWHC
2930 McClure St. Suite 201
Oakland, Cal. 94609
415-444-5676

Orange County FWHC
429 S. Sycamore St.
Santa Ana, Cal. 92707
714-547-0327

Emma Goldman Clinic
715 N. Dodge
Iowa City, Iowa 52240

Women's Clinic
801 N. Cascade
Colorado Springs, Colo.

Salt Lake City Women's
    Center
363 E. 6th Street
Salt Lake City, Utah

Women's Health &
    Information Project
Box 110 Warriner
C.M.U.
Mt. Pleasant, Mich. 48858

Women's Health Collective
c/o Ann Shalleck
100 E. Cleveden
Philadelphia, Pa.

Chico FWHC
330 Flume St.
Chico, Cal. 95926
916-342-0944

Detroit FWHC
2445 W. 8 Mile Rd.
Detroit, Mich. 48203
313-892-7790

Salt Lake City FWHC
363 East 6th St.
Salt Lake City, Utah 84404
801-328-3032

Tallahassee FWHC
1126 Lee Ave.
Tallahassee, Fla. 32303
904-244-9441

Berkeley Women's Health
    Collective
2908 Ellsworth
Berkeley, Cal.
415-843-6194

Jacksonville Self-Help
c/o Joan Edelson
1232 Laura Street
Jacksonville, Fla. 32206

Suggested Reading

ABORTION AND THE LAW

Constitutional Aspects of the Right to Limit Childbearing. United States Commission on Human Rights, April 1975.

Ross, Susan C., *The Rights of Women.* New York: Avon Books, 1973.

MEDICAL ASPECTS OF ABORTION

Gutcheon, Beth Richardson, *Abortion: A Woman's Guide.* Planned Parenthood, New York: Abelard-Schuman, 1973.

Boston Women's Health Collective, *Our Bodies, Ourselves.* New York: Simon and Schuster, 1973.

Vacuum Aspiration Abortion and *Saline Abortion.* (pamphlets) Women's Health Forum, 156 5th Avenue, New York, New York 10010.

ALTERNATIVES

Whelan, Elizabeth M., *A Baby? ... Maybe.* New York: Bobbs-Merrill, 1975.

Woolley, Persia, *Creative Survival for Single Mothers.* Millbrae, CA: Celestial Arts, 1975.

Hope, Karol, and Nancy Young, eds., *Momma Handbook: Sourcebook for Single Mothers.* New York: New American Library, 1976.

Rollin, Betty, *Motherhood, Who Needs It?* National Organization for Non-Parents, 806 Reistertown Rd., Baltimore, MD 21208.

Fried, John, *Vastectomy: Truth or Consequences.* Benwood, WV: Pyramid Press Publishing Company, 1974.

PREVENTION

Elwin, Verrier, *Kingdom of the Young.* New York: Oxford University Press, 1968.

Cherniak, Donna and Allan Feingold, *The Birth Control Handbook.* Montreal Health Press Inc., 1973. P. O. Box 1000, Station G, Montreal 130, Quebec, H2W2N1, Canada. 25¢ for mailing.

Lader, Lawrence, ed., *Foolproof Birth Control: Male and Female Steriliza-tion*. Beacon Press, 1972.

Lacey, Louise, *Lunaception*. New York: Coward, McCann, and Geoghe-gan Inc., 1975.

Ostrander, Sheila and Lyn Schroeder, *Natural Birth Control*. New York: Bantam Books, 1973.

Nofziger, Margaret, *Natural Birth Control*. (pamphlet) The Farm, Sum-mertown, TN 38483. 25¢ for mailing.

Rosenblum, Art, *Natural Birth Control Book*. Aquarian Research Founda-tion, 5620 Morton Street, Philadelphia, PA 19144. $3.00.

Billings, John, *Natural Family Planning, The Ovulation Method*. College-ville, MN: Liturgical Press, 1975.

Boston Women's Health Collective, *Our Bodies, Ourselves*. New York: Simon and Schuster, 1976.

Hammond, Karen Faire, *Natural Methods of Conception and Contracep-tion*. (booklet) Karen Faire Hammond, Box 103, Bodega, CA 94922.

SEXUALITY

Barbach, Lonnie Garfield, *For Yourself: The Fulfillment of Female Sexu-ality*. New York: Signet Classics, 1976.

Rush, Anne Kent, *Getting Clear: Body Work for Women*. New York: Ran-dom House, 1973.

Masters, William H. and Virginia E. Johnson, *Human Sexual Response*. Boston: Little, Brown, and Company, 1966.

Kaplan, Helen, *The New Sex Therapy*. New York: Brunner-Mazel, 1973.

Keleman, Stanley, *Sexuality, Self, and Survival*. San Francisco: Lodestar Press, 1971.

Rosenberg, Jack Lee, *Total Orgasm*. New York: Random House, 1976.

Montagu, Ashley, *Touching*. New York: Harper and Row, 1972.

SEXUALITY-TEENAGERS

Lyvely, Chin, and Joyce Sutton, *Abortion Eve*. Nanny Goat Productions, P.O. Box 845, Laguna Beach, CA 92652. 75¢.

Southard, Helen F., *Sex Before Twenty: New Answers for Youth*. New York: E. P. Dutton and Company, 1971.

Fiore, Evelyn and Richard S. Ward, *Sex Facts for Teenagers*. New York: Ace Books, 1971.

Liberman, James E. and Ellen Peck, *Sex, Love, and Birth Control: A Guide for the Young.* New York: Thomas Y. Crowell Company, 1973.

Pierce, Ruth I., *Single and Pregnant.* Boston: Beacon Press, 1971.

SELF DEVELOPMENT

Singer, June, *Boundaries of the Soul.* New York: Doubleday and Company, 1973.

Mander, Anica Vesel and Anne Kent Rush, *Feminism as Therapy.* New York: Random House, 1974.

Granger, Peggy, *Everywoman's Guide to a New Image.* Millbrae, CA: Les Femmes Publishing, 1976.

Rush, Anne Kent, *Getting Clear: Body Work for Women.* New York: Random House, 1976.

Bloomfield, Harold H., *Happiness, the TM Program, Psychiatry, and Enlightenment.* New York: Dawn Press, 1976.

Taubman, Bryna, *How To Become an Assertive Woman.* New York: Pocket Books, 1976.

Castellejo, Irene Claremont de, *Knowing Woman.* New York: Putnam, 1973.

Downing, George, *Massage.* New York: Random House, 1972.

New Women's Survival Catalogue. New York: Cowen, McCann, and Geoghegan.

McWilliams, Peter, and Denise Dennis, *The TM Book: How to Enjoy the Rest of Your Life.* New York: Warner Books, 1975.

PROFESSIONAL

Pierce, Ruth, *Single and Pregnant.* Boston: Beacon Press, 1971.

Luker, Kristen, *Taking Chances: Abortion and the Decision Not to Contracept.* Berkeley: University of California Press, 1975.

American Friends Service Committee, *Who Shall Live? Man's Control Over Birth and Death.* New York: Hill and Wang, 1970.

Women's Educational Project, *High School Sexuality, A Teaching Guide.* Amazon Reality Collective, P. O. Box 95, Eugene, OR 97401. $1.00.

Keller, Christa and Pamela Copeland, *Counseling the Abortion Patient is More Than Talk.* Reprinted from *The American Journal of Nursing,* Jan. 1972, vol. 72, no. 1, 1972. Available from Association for the Study of Abortion, Inc., 120 W. 57th Street, New York, New York 10019.

SELF-HELP/WOMEN'S HEALTH COLLECTIVE

Circle One Self Health Handbook. Women's Health Center, 409 E. Fontanero, Colorado Springs, CO 80907. 75¢.

Healthright. (Newsletter of the women's health movement) 175 5th Avenue, New York, New York 10010.

West Coast Sisters, *How to Start Your Self Help Clinic, Level II.* Self Help Clinic One, 946 Crenshaw Blvd., Los Angeles, CA 90005.

Hirsh, Lolly, ed., *The Monthly Extract.* New Moon Publications, Box 3488, Ridgeway Station, Stamford, CT 06905.

Source Collective, *Organizing for Health Care: A Tool for Change.* New York: Beacon Press, 1974.

Ehrenreich, Barbara and Deidre English, *Witches, Midwives, and Nurses, A History of Women Healers.* Glass Mountain Pamphlets, The Feminist Press, Box 334, Old Westbury, New York 11568.

Cowan, Belita, *Women and Health Care: Resources, Writing, Bibliography.* 556 2nd Avenue, Ann Arbor, MI, $3.00.

The Abortion Business: A Report on Freestanding Abortion Clinics. Women's Research Action Project, Box 119, Porter Square Station, Cambridge, MA 02140. 35¢.

PARENTING

Fraiberg, Selma H., *The Magic Years.* New York: Scribner, 1968.

Leonard, George B., *Education and Ecstasy.* New York: Dell Publishing Company, 1968.

Dreikhurs, Rudolph and Vicki Soltz, *Children: The Challenge.* New York: Hawthorn Books, Inc., 1964.

Skolnick, Arlene S. and Jerome S. Skolnick, *Family in Transition: Rethinking Marriage, Sex, Child Rearing, and Family Organization.* Boston: Little Brown, Inc., 1971.

Geddes, Joan Bel, *How to Parent Alone: A Guide for Single Parents.* New York: Arco Publishing Company, Inc., 1974.

Beller, Harry and Dennis Meredith, *Father Power.* New York: David McKay, 1975.

National Organization for Non-Parents, 806 Reisterstown Road, Baltimore, MD 21208.

Woolley, Persia, *Creative Survival for Single Mothers.* Millbrae, CA: Celestial Arts, 1976.

INSPIRATION

Morgan, Elaine, *Descent of Woman*. New York: Bantam Books, 1973.

Nin, Anais, *Diary I-V*. New York: Harcourt, Brace, Jovanovich, Inc.

Mead, Margaret, *Male and Female*. New York: Dell Publishing Company, 1970.

Dillard, Annie, *Pilgrim At Tinker Creek*. New York: Bantam Books, 1975.

Chicago, Judy, *Through the Flower*. New York: Doubleday, 1973.

Lerner, Gerda, *The Woman in American History*. Menlo Park, CA: Addison-Wesley, 1971.

Radl, Shirley L., *Mothers Day is Over*. New York: Warner Books, 1974.

Sheehy, Gail, *Passages*. New York: Dutton, 1976.

Gordon, Linda, *Woman's Body, Woman's Right: Birth Control in America*. New York: Viking, 1976.

Shapiro, Howard I., *The Birth Control Book*. New York: St. Martin's Press, 1977.

Hutches, Robert et al, *Contraceptive Technology 1976-1977*. New York: Irvington Publishers, 1976.

Bibliography

American Friends Service Committee, *Who Shall Live? Man's Control over Birth and Death.* New York: Hill and Wang, 1970.

Barbach, Lonnie Garfield, *For Yourself: The Fulfillment of Female Sexuality.* New York: Signet Classics, 1976.

Billings, John, *Natural Family Planning, The Ovulation Method.* Collegeville, MI: Liturgical Press, 1975.

Bloomfield, Harold H. M.D. and Richard Kory, *Happiness, The TM Program and Enlightenment.* New York: Dawn Press/Simon & Schuster, 1976.

Boston Women's Health Collective, *Our Bodies Ourselves.* New York: Simon & Schuster, 1976.

Castaneda, Carlos, *Tales of Power.* New York: Simon & Schuster, 1976.

Cherniak, Donna and Allan Feingold, *The Birth Control Handbook.* Montreal, Quebec: Health Press Inc., 1973.

Chester, Phyllis, *Women and Madness.* New York: Doubleday, 1972.

Chicago, Judy, *Through the Flower.* New York: Doubleday, 1973.

Constitutional Aspects of the Right to Limit Childbearing, A report of the United States Commission on Civil Rights, April 1975.

de Castellejo, Irene, *Knowing Woman.* New York: G. P. Putnam's Sons, 1973.

Devereux, George, *A Study of Abortion in Primitive Societies.* New York: International University Press, 1955 rev. 1975.

"Digest: Find D & E is Safest Method of Midtrimester Abortion, But Saline is Less Risky than Prostaglandins: JPSA," *Family Planning Perspectives.* Vol. 8, no. 6, Dec. 1976.

Ekblad, Martin, "Induced Abortion on Psychiatric Grounds: A Followup Study of 479 Women." *Acta Psyciatrica Neurologica Scandinavica.* Supplement 99, 1955.

Elwin, Verrier, *Kingdom of the Young.* England: Oxford University Press.

Epstein, Dr. Samuel, "Birth Defects and Thier Environmental Causes," *Medical World News.* McGraw-Hill Publications, Jan. 22, 1971.

Erlich, Paul, "The Population Explosion Facts and Fiction," *Sierra Club Bulletin*, Oct. 1968.

Fiore, Evelyn and Richard S. Ward, *Sex Facts for Teenagers*. New York: Ace Books, 1971.

Feldman, David M., *Birth Control in Jewish Law*. New York: New York University Press, 1968.

Flanagan, Geraldine, *First Nine Months of Life*. New York: Simon & Schuster, 1962.

Gardner, R. F. R., *Abortion, The Personal Dilemma*. New York: Pyramid Books, 1974.

Gaskin, Ina May, *Spiritual Midwifery*. Summertown, TN: The Book Publishing Co., 1975.

Gaylor, Anne Nicol, *Abortion is a Blessing*. New York: Psychological Dimensions Inc., 1975.

Gilbert, Margaret Shea, *Biography of the Unborn*. New York: Hafner Publications Co., 1962.

Granger, Peggy, *Everywoman's Guide to a New Image*. Millbrae, CA: Les Femmes, 1976.

Gutcheon, Beth Richardson, *Abortion: A Woman's Guide*. New York: Abelard-Schuman, 1973.

Hammond, Karen Faire, *Natural Methods of Conception and Contraception*. Bodega, CA: unpublished, 1976.

Hardin, Garrett, *Mandatory Motherhood*. Boston: Beacon Press, 1974.

Harding, Esther, *Psychic Energy: Its Source and Its Transformation*. New York: Random House/Pantheon Books, 1963.

Harding, Esther, *Way of All Women*. New York: B. P. Putnam's Sons, 1971.

Harding, Esther, *Woman's Mysteries: A Psychological Interpretation of the Feminine Principle as Portrayed in Myth, Story and Dreams*. New York: G. P. Putnam's Sons, 1971.

Hirsh, Lolly, *The Monthly Extract*. Stamford, CT: New Moon Publications, Vol. 5, Issue 2, July/August 1976.

Hope, Karol and Nancy Young, *Momma: The Sourcebook for Single Mothers*. New York: New American Library, 1976.

Keller, Christa and Pamela Copeland, "Counseling the Abortion Patient is More than Talk," *The American Journal of Nursing*. Vol. 72, no. 1, Jan. 1972.

144

Kimmey, Jimmye, *Legal Abortion, A Speakers Noteboo* ciation for the Study of Abortion, Inc.

Konopka, Gisela, *Adolescent Girl in Conflict.* Engl Prentice-Hall, Inc., 1966.

Lacey, Louise, *Lunaception.* New York: Coward, McCann and Geoghegan Inc., 1975.

Lader, Lawrence, ed., *Foolproof Birth Control: Male and Female Steriliza-tion.* Boston: Beacon Press, 1972.

Lerner, Gerda, *The Woman in American History.* Menlo Park, CA: Addi-son-Wesley, 1971.

Liberman, James E., and Ellen Peck, *Sex, Love, and Birth Control: A Guide for the Young,* New York: Thomas Y. Crowell Co., 1973.

Luker, Kristen, *Taking Chances, Abortion and the Decision Not to Contra-cept.* Berkeley: University of California Press, 1975.

Lyvely, Chin and Joyce Sutton, *Abortion Eve.* Laguna Beach, Nanny Goat Productions, 1973.

Mander, Anica Vesel and Anne Kent Rush, *Feminism as Therapy.* New York: Random House, 1974.

Maslow, Abraham, *Toward a Psychology of Being.* Princeton: Van Nostrand, 1968, 2nd ed.

Masters, William H., and Virginia E. Johnson, *Human Sexual Response.* Boston: Little, Brown, & Co., 1966.

McWilliams, Peter, and Denise Denniston, *The TM Book, How to Enjoy the Rest of Your Life.* Allen Park, MI: Versemonger Press, 1975.

Means, C. in *Abortion: Law, Choice, and Morality* by Daniel Callahan. New York: The Macmillan Co., 1972.

Miller, Jean Baker, *Toward a New Psychology of Women.* Boston: Beacon Press, 1976.

Mills, Don Harper, "Prenatal Diethylstilbestrol and Vaginal Cancer in Offspring." *Journal of the American Medical Association,* Vol. 229. No. 4, (July 22, 1974).

Montagu, Ashley, *Touching.* New York: Harper & Row, 1972.

Neumann, Erich, *The Child.* New York: Harper & Row, 1976.

Nin, Anais, *The Diary of Anais Nin.* New York: Harcourt, Brace, Jovanovich, 1976.

Nofziger, Margaret, *Natural Birth Control.* Summertown, TN: The Book Publishing Co., 1976.

Oates, Robert M., Jr., *Celebrating the Dawn*. New York: G. P. Putnam's Sons, 1977.

Ostrander, Sheila and Lyn Schroeder, *Natural Birth Control*. New York: Bantam Books, 1973.

Paulshock, Bernadine, "Birth Control: What I Want My Daughter to Know" *Today's Health*. Feb., 1975.

Pierce, Ruth I. *Single and Pregnant*. Boston: Beacon Press, 1971.

"Remarkable American Women 1776-1976," *Life Special Report*.

Richards, Mary Caroline, *Centering in Pottery, Poetry and the Person*. Middletown: Wesleyan University Press, 1962.

Richardson, John A., and Geoffrey Dixon, *British Medical Journal*, 1 (6021), May 29, 1976, p. 1303-1304.

Rollin, Betty, "Motherhood, Who Needs It?" Baltimore, MD: National Organization for Non-Parents.

Rosenblum, Art, *Natural Birth Control Book*. Philadephia, PA: Aquarian Research Foundation, 1974.

Rosoff, Jeannie I., *Planned Parenthood—World Population Washington Memo*. July 2, 1976.

Ross, Susan C., *The Rights of Women*. New York: Avon Books, 1973.

Rush, Anne Kent, *Getting Clear: Body Work for Women*. New York: Random House, 1973.

Seaman, Barbara, *Free and Female*. New York: Coward, McCann & Geoghegan, 1972.

Seaman, Barbara, *The Doctors' Case Against the Pill*. New York: Peter H. Wyden, Inc., 1969.

Singer, June, *Boundaries of the Soul: The Practice of Jung's Psychology*. Garden City, NY: Doubleday, 1973.

Southard, Helen F., *Sex Before Twenty: New Answers for Youth*. New York: E. P. Dutton Co., 1971.

Summerhill, Louise, *The Story of Birthright, The Alternative to Abortion*. Kenosha, WI: Prow Books, 1973.

Taubman, Byrna, *How To Become An Assertive Woman*. New York: Pocket Books, 1976.

Troeller, Gordon and Claude Deffarge, *Stern*. August, 1972.

Wallerstein, Judith, *et al*, "Psychosocial Sequelae of Therapeutic Abortion in Young Unmarried Women," *Archives of General Psychiatry*, Vol. 27, Dec. 1972.

West Coast Sisters, *How To Start Your Self Help Clinic, Level II.* Los Angeles, CA: Self Help Clinic One, 1971.

Whelan, Dr. Elizabeth M., *A Baby? . . . Maybe.* New York: Bobbs-Merrill Co., 1975.

Women's Educational Project, *High School Sexuality—A Teaching Guide.* Eugene, OR: Amazon Reality Collective, 1974.

Women's Health Center, *Circle One Self Health Handbook.* Colorado Springs, CO: Women's Health Center, 1972.

Women's Health Forum, *Vacuum Aspiration Abortion* and *Saline Abortion.* New York.

Woolley, Persia, *Creative Survival for Single Mothers.* Millbrae, CA: Celestial Arts, 1976.

EVERYWOMAN'S GUIDE SERIES

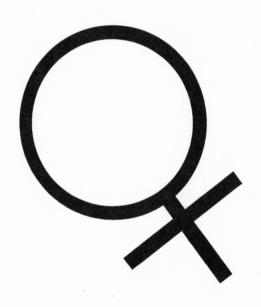

EVERYWOMAN'S GUIDE TO TIME MANAGEMENT
Donna Goldfein
128 pages $3.95

A back-to-basics, step-by-step program tailored for the woman –
homemaker or professional – who is bogged down by routine
and wants to take charge of her life. The reader will learn to
establish priorities, set time limits, schedule realistically, communicate effectively, simplify tasks, systematize, delegate, and
anticipate problems. "Practical...innovative."---*Booklist.*

EVERYWOMAN'S GUIDE TO TRAVEL
Donna Goldfein
128 pages $3.95

How to get all the excitement, glamour, freedom, relaxation,
pleasure, and privacy traveling can offer. The author shares
her years of travel experience in an indispensable guide that
will help both novice and seasoned traveler enjoy the special
sense of freedom and release from routine that traveling offers.
Special chapters deal with international and emergency travel.
"Everything a woman should know about getting the most out
of going places the easiest."---*Chicago Sun-Times.*

EVERYWOMAN'S GUIDE TO POLITICAL AWARENESS
Phyllis Butler and Dorothy Gray
128 pages $3.95

This is a fact-filled handbook for all women who want a positive
introduction to institutional and power politics. It reviews the political structure, types of activity (volunteer, political pro, candidate)
how to get involved, basic do's and don'ts, the running of a campaign, and much more.

EVERYWOMAN'S GUIDE TO FINANCIAL INDEPENDENCE
Mavis Arthur Groza
144 pages $3.95

Rich or poor, single or married, every woman's questions about how
to handle finances are answered in this comprehensive money book.
It covers investing, budgeting, credit, insurance, estate planning,
saving and security, as well as the new credit laws and government
programs affecting the monetary concerns of women.

BOOKS OF RELATED INTEREST

In CONVERSATIONS: WORKING WOMEN TALK ABOUT DOING A "MAN'S JOB", Terry Wetherby conducts frank interviews with women who have succeeded in traditionally male occupations. Included are a biochemist with the Viking space project, Top Fuel race car driver Shirley Muldowney and twenty others. 288 pages, soft cover, $4.95

Antoinette May's DIFFERENT DRUMMERS: THEY DID WHAT THEY WANTED contains biographies of six celebrated risk-takers. None of these fascinating women was content merely to hear the faint tattoo of a different drummer -- each was determined to own the drum! 160 pages, soft cover, $4.95

Far from being limited to women, the Equal Rights Amendment (ERA) will dramatically affect 100% of the population, both directly and indirectly. IMPACT ERA is the first and only book to predict ways in which the ERA will affect individual rights, employment, education, and domestic relations, both legally and socially. Edited by the California Commission on the Status of Women. 288 pages, soft cover, $4.95

CRIMES AGAINST WOMEN documents the shocking testimony heard by the International Tribunal on Crimes Against Women held in Brussels in March, 1976. Diana E.H. Russell and Nicole Van de Ven brilliantly re-create the incidents, record the moving personal accounts of appalling physical and mental brutality, discuss the resolutions and proposals for change, analyze the media's response, and assess the impact of the five incredible days when international feminism was born. 320 pages, soft cover, $5.95

Dramatic true stories of women who helped shape the American West are recounted by Dorothy Gray in WOMEN OF THE WEST. 160 pages, soft cover, $5.95

An exciting introduction to the world of women and art is to be found in WOMEN AND CREATIVITY. Rejecting the myth that there have been no great women artists, Joelynn Snyder-Ott reveals in words and photographs the lasting contributions of women to the world of art from the time of the pre-Christian fertility cults to the present day. 160 pages, soft cover, $5.95

Available at your local book or department store or directly from the publisher. To order by mail, send check or money order to:

Les Femmes Publishing
231 Adrian Road
Suite MPB
Millbrae, California 94030

Please include 50 cents for postage and handling. California residents add 6% tax.